poké

hardie grant books

Celia Farrar
and
Guy Jackson

POKĔ

Photography by
Matt Russell

Hawaiian-inspired
sushi bowls

Contents

Introduction

Aloha!
Thank you for buying our book. Before you dive into our delicious sea of recipes, we'd like to introduce ourselves: Celia Farrar and Guy Jackson, two Londoners who fell in love with poke - pronounced poh-kay.

Pathway to Poke

Our poke story began in 2012. On a trip to LA, Celia was taken to a local hole-in-the-wall spot called Poke Poke on Venice Beach, where the team were doling out pots of delicious marinated fish to a hungry queue of surfers, skaters and locals.

After teaming up with fellow food enthusiast Guy, we began thinking about how we could bring this sunny, laid-back attitude to London. After months of obsessive research and recipe testing (and a cheeky trip to Hawaii) we started Eat Poke, London's first poke eatery, trading with Kerb, Street Feast and Druid Street food markets.

Now we want to share our poke with you. With Celia's background in fashion and Guy's in branding, design plays an important role in our dishes and the look of our first recipe book. We hope you enjoy creating these vibrant, healthy and seriously tasty tropical bowls.

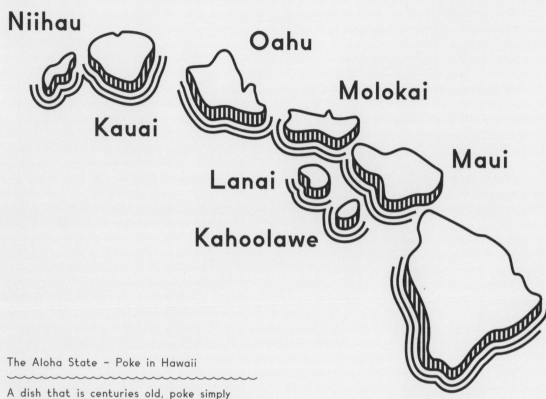

Niihau

Oahu

Molokai

Kauai

Maui

Lanai

Kahoolawe

Hawaii

The Aloha State - Poke in Hawaii

A dish that is centuries old, poke simply means 'to cut' or 'section' and traditionally consists of chunks of fresh, raw fish, served sprinkled with Hawaiian sea salt and mixed with crunchy local limu seaweed. Hawaiian cuisine is an exhilarating melting pot of culinary influences. Walk into any supermarket or local convenience store in Hawaii and chances are you will find row upon row of fresh poke, featuring flavour profiles from across the Pacific, Asia and Europe. During our visits to the islands, we would spend hours sampling and chatting away to the hugely welcoming and knowledgeable store owners. At one such place, the family-run Alicia's Market in Honolulu, Alicia's grandson talked us through the fresh Hawaiian delicacies on offer and sorted us out with some of the best poke we had ever had.

Although inspired by the poke we have tasted in Hawaii and Los Angeles (tough job, but somebody had to do it), our poke is firmly non-traditional – if we like the idea of it, in it goes. The key, really, is just to select the freshest ingredients available to you. As well as poke bowls, we have widened the scope of the recipes in this book to include small plates and all the tasty extras that we use to pimp our poke. This includes plenty of ideas for pickles, a bit of an obsession of ours, alongside some Hawaiian classics, such as Lomi Lomi Salmon (page 46).

Poke bowls are extremely customisable to suit specific tastes and dietary requirements: if catering for vegetarians sub out the tuna in our Tropical Ahi Poke (page 35) for chopped avocado and cubes of cooked sweet potato, or replace the rice with shredded spring greens. We like to think of poke as a more easy-going version of sushi, and we would encourage you to mix and match with the recipes that follow. Choose local, seasonal produce, pick a marinade, throw in a pickle or crunchy topping and suddenly you have created your own bowl of sunshine.

Olakino
Maika'i

↓

To
live
healthy

A Note on Sourcing

For most people, the idea of sourcing and handling raw fish is the most intimidating part of creating any poke dish. Our advice? Make friends with your fishmonger! When we started out, Sam, our local fishmonger at Jonathan Norris in Victoria Park, London, proved an indispensable fountain of knowledge about selecting and preparing the freshest fish to eat raw. He has shared some of his top tips with us on pages 20–21, along with a handy illustrated guide to help you get started on filleting fish.

Next up, is a responsibility we all have: to make ethical and sustainable choices when consuming fish. Again, your fishmonger should be your first port of call here, while goodfishguide.org is a useful online guide on choosing sustainable seafood.

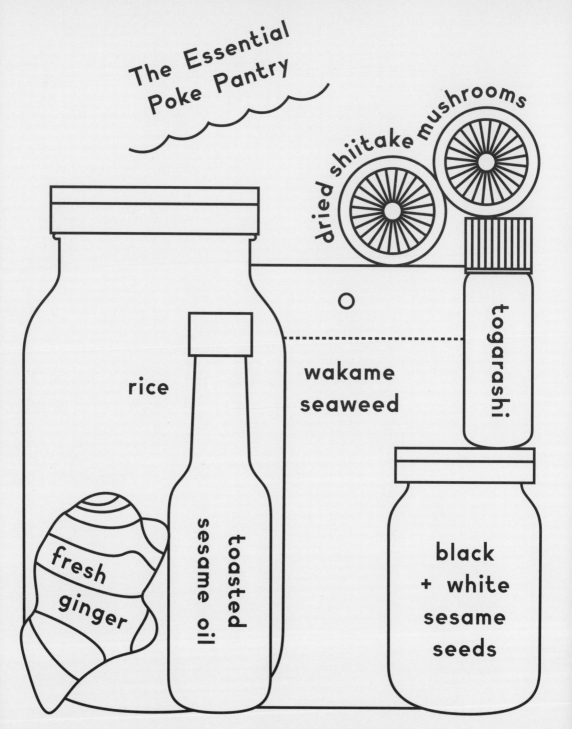

The Essential Poke Pantry

dried shiitake mushrooms

togarashi

rice

wakame seaweed

toasted sesame oil

fresh ginger

black + white sesame seeds

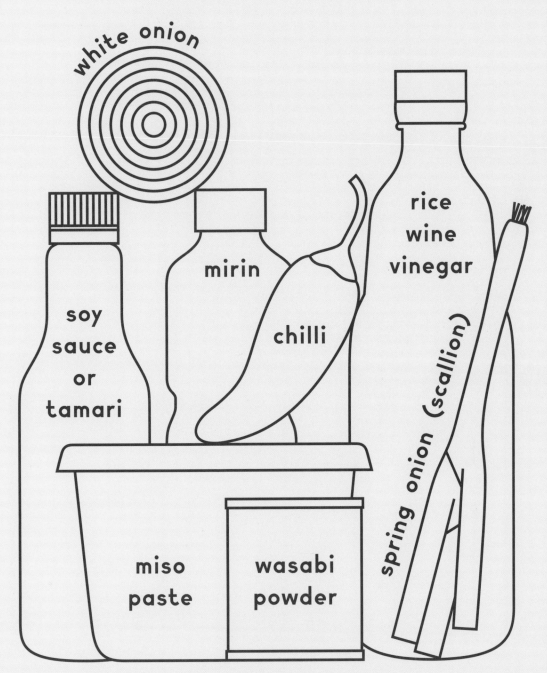

white onion

rice wine vinegar

mirin

chilli

soy sauce or tamari

spring onion (scallion)

miso paste

wasabi powder

13

The Pro
Poke Pantry

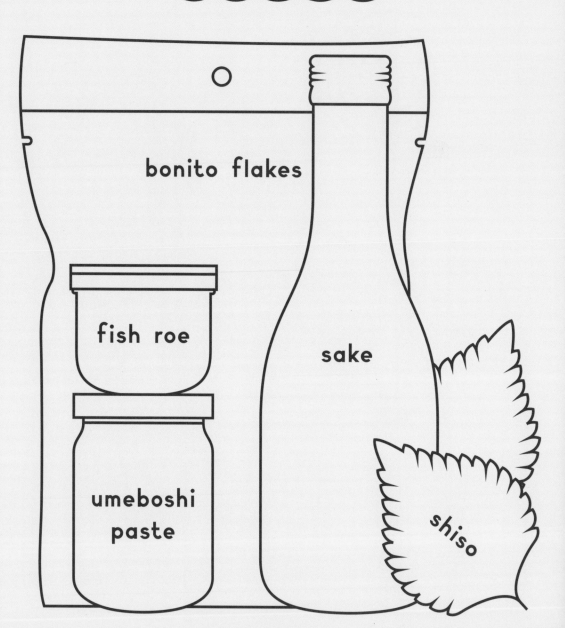

bonito flakes

fish roe

sake

umeboshi
paste

shiso

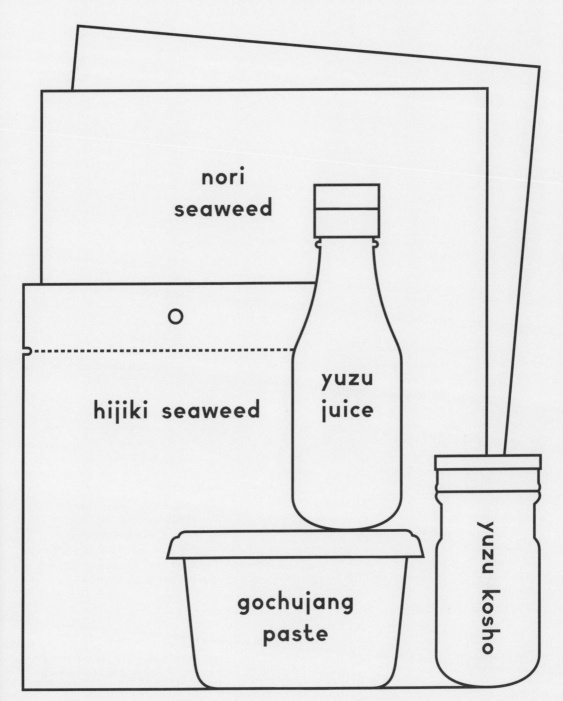

nori
seaweed

hijiki seaweed

yuzu
juice

gochujang
paste

yuzu kosho

For us, there is nothing more exciting than getting lost within the rows of magical ingredients at our local Asian supermarket. But this isn't always practical! So we have compiled a pantry to help you find the essentials for making poke. We have also extended the list for the more intrepid – dare ya!

The Essential Poke Pantry

Black + White Sesame Seeds
Little pearls of joy. Almost as important as soy sauce in our poke recipes. To keep them fresh, store in an airtight container or sealable jar.

Chilli
Red, green, whatever – always have some to hand to help power up your poke. We use bird's eyes, habaneros and jalapeños, but you can use another variety if you prefer.

Dried Shiitake Mushrooms
These add so much umami. Once hydrated, these meaty mushrooms can be used for stocks, pickles or as the star of a dish.

Fresh Ginger
A must. Fresh as it can be and as much of it as you can handle. It features in most of our recipes for good reason. It cleanses the palate and adds a fiery kick.

Mirin
A sweet rice wine, with a mild acidity. A key ingredient for seasoning rice (page 25).

Miso Paste
This is made from fermented soy beans. We use both sweet white miso and salty red miso.

Rice
An obvious staple! We often use a short-grain variety, normally labelled as sushi rice. Alternative types we use are brown and black.

Rice Wine Vinegar
A mild vinegar made from rice. Ideal for Japanese salad dressings and pickles. It is less acidic than other vinegars such as sherry, distilled white vinegar and some wine vinegars.

Soy Sauce or Tamari (gluten-free)
We could drink this stuff – definitely have! We prefer a lighter style. Tamari is a gluten-free version we also use.

Spring Onion (scallions)
We use both the white and the green ends of our oniony friends. They help to season our dishes with subtle onion undertones.

Toasted Sesame Oil
Wonderfully strong oil. You only need to buy a small bottle: a little goes a long way, so it is worth paying for a good-quality oil.

Togarashi Powder
A spicy seasoning made from a famous Japanese blend of seven flavours, which adds a glorious kick.

Wakame Seaweed
A type of dried seaweed. It is available from most specialist stores. We use it in salads and soups.

Wasabi Powder
Japanese horseradish packs a punch. We recommend brands with at least 4 per cent wasabi. It needs to be mixed with water before use.

White Onion
Ideally, get the sweetest you can find. In Hawaii, Maui onion is traditionally used – it adds crunch and sweetness to poke bowls.

The Pro Poke Pantry

Bonito Flakes
Dried and fermented skipjack tuna shavings – far tastier than they sound! Use to add depth of flavour to soups or sprinkle over poke bowls.

Fish Roe (flying fish roe)
Tobiko, masago and ikura are the most commonly used fish roe for poke and sushi. We love tobiko for its smoky taste and crunchy texture.

Gochujang Paste
A punchy Korean hot pepper paste – a little goes a long way! Also comes as flakes known as gochugaru.

Hijiki Seaweed
Edible seaweed, used along with bonito flakes to add umami depth to dashi stock.

Nori Seaweed
Dark green sheets of edible seaweed, most commonly used in sushi. Its saltiness is a great addition to a dish. Also available in shredded form called Kizami Nori.

Sake
Brewed Japanese rice wine. They come in lots of varieties and, depending on the grade; it is drunk warm or cold.

Shiso
A ridiculously good-looking Asian herb. With its unique, delicate fragrance, this is sometimes likened to mint or basil. We use it in furikake seasonings, poke dishes and infused oils.

Umeboshi Paste
This versatile, tangy and slightly salty Japanese condiment is made from dried, pickled ume (plum) fruits. We use it to add a tartness to our dressings and mayos.

Yuzu Juice
A sour Japanese citrus juice that's widely available bottled from larger supermarket. You can substitute it with the juice of other citrus fruits, but it's not quite the same.

Yuzu Kosho (chilli paste)
A salty, spicy paste made from fermented chilli peppers and yuzu fruit peel.

Building a Poke Bowl

Right... time to get started. To give you an idea of how we build our poke bowls, we have created a handy illustration (see opposite). Poke is a relaxed, laid-back style of food, so follow this spirit and don't be afraid to freestyle and find your own way – mixing pimps, salads or even fish.

A few things to remember: the fish is the star of the show, so source it carefully and be generous. Choose a wide bowl, pile it high and get stuck in!

1 – Base

If you want a base, then white rice would be the most traditional option. However, we prefer brown or black rice for its awesome taste and texture, along with its extra health benefits. Not all of our recipes call for rice – you can use all sorts of grains, noodles or vegetables. Give it a go and find your favourite.

2 – Salad

We love the extra freshness you get from a seasonal salad. It adds flavour, colour and crunch to the dish. For us, salads are a key part of our poke. They allow us to be more inventive and playful.

3 – Protein

The main show! The best bit, some say! We use a variety of fish from the island, from classic ahi (tuna) to scallops. The fresher the better! We also have a number of vegan and vegetarian alternatives to suit all.

4 – Marinade

This is what helps differentiate poke from sushi or sashimi. Generally in most modern and traditional poke recipes the fish is marinated. This helps to add depth and flavour to the fish.

5 – Pimps

A pimp has many connotations, but for us it is the glorious extras that add a new dimension to your poke. These are not always necessary, but are worth the effort.

6 – Toppings and Seasoning

The cherry on top! Toppings and seasonings are the fancy bits. Our favourites without a doubt are furikake (pages 90-93) – these add extra depth, crunch and flavour, and they also look beautiful.

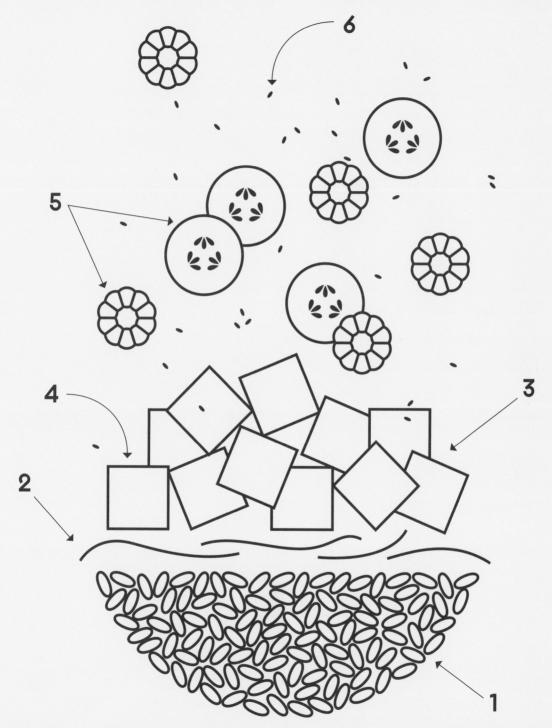

Choosing Fish for Poke

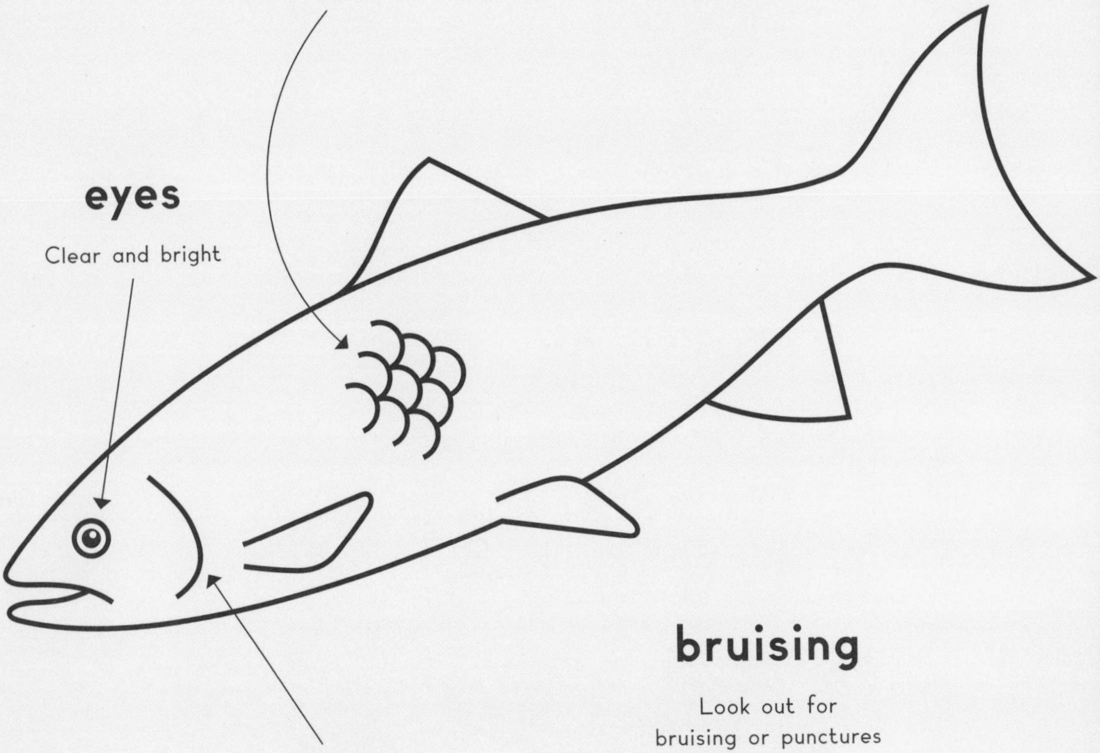

scales

Shouldn't pull off easily

smell

Shouldn't smell fishy

eyes

Clear and bright

bruising

Look out for bruising or punctures to the skin

gills

Should be bright and red

Selecting an appropriate fish can seem like a daunting task at first; however, choosing and preparing fish is a very satisfying process. Start at your nearest fishmonger and check out their selection. It is important to build a relationship with your fishmonger and let them know what you intend to do with the fish, especially if you plan to eat it raw.

We have a great relationship with our local fishmonger: Sam from Jonathan Norris in Victoria Park Village, London. He is always recommending whatever is in season and pushing us to try something new. Ideally, we call ahead to make specific requests. Unless your supermarket has a fish counter, we would not advise making poke with fish from the supermarket.

In theory, you can eat almost all fish raw. We would recommend starting with a fish you are familiar with and building confidence – but always ask your fishmonger's advice.

We have worked with our man Sam to come up with a few pointers to help you:

Equipment

Make like a sushi surgeon and get those knives sharp!

- Filleting knife
  This has a flexible blade that allows you to cut easily between the bones and the flesh of the fish. We highly recommend sharpening it before starting; it will make it a lot easier and help with your yield
- Fish bone tweezers
- Plastic chopping board
- Clean wiping cloths
- Knife sharpener
- Scissors
- Bandana (optional)

Preparing a fish

Depending on your level of fish-prepping confidence and experience, you can normally ask your fishmonger to do any of the following:

- Descale your fish (although if you are going to skin it at home, leave the scales on)
- Remove the internal bits and pieces (but keep the roe if there is any – it is yum)
- Fillet the fish
- Debone (you might get a grunt at this)

If you're going to prep and fillet your fish at home, follow our step-by-step guide overleaf.

The most important thing is not to worry. Filleting fish is definitely something you get better at over time as your confidence grows. We started our filleting education on YouTube – so if we can do it, anyone can! Most round fish can be filleted following the simple steps below.

Prepping Fish for Poke

Step 1

Prepare like a boss! Make sure your working space, utensils and chopping boards are all clean and ready.

Step 2 (fig 1)

Hold the whole fish by the head, belly towards you. Using the tip of the knife, pierce the stomach of the fish, just under the chin. Run the knife from the head down the length of the fish, cutting open the stomach.

Step 3

Discard the innards and rinse out the cavity of the fish under cold running water. Make sure your fishy friend is nice and clean. Once happy, pat dry and return to the chopping board.

Step 4 (fig 2)

Just beside the head but to the left of the pectoral fin, make a deep, angular cut towards the head. Cut down until you hit the bone. Then turn the knife towards the tail, preparing to cut the fillet off.

Step 5

Run the knife down the spine to the tail using long, smooth cuts. The aim is to get the blade to cut gently between the spine and the flesh.

Step 6 (fig 3)

Repeat this motion all the way to the tail – the fillet should begin to come away. It can be easier to lift the fillet at this point, so you can see where you are cutting. Once the fillet is free, place it to the side.

Step 7

Turn the fish over and repeat this action with the second fillet. The second fillet can be a little tricky, but with patience and confidence, you will prevail!

Step 8 (fig 4)

Remove the skin from the fillets. Place the fillets skin side down on a chopping board. Begin by holding the fillet by the tail, then run the knife between the skin and the flesh, all the way down. Keep a tight hold of the skin during this process.

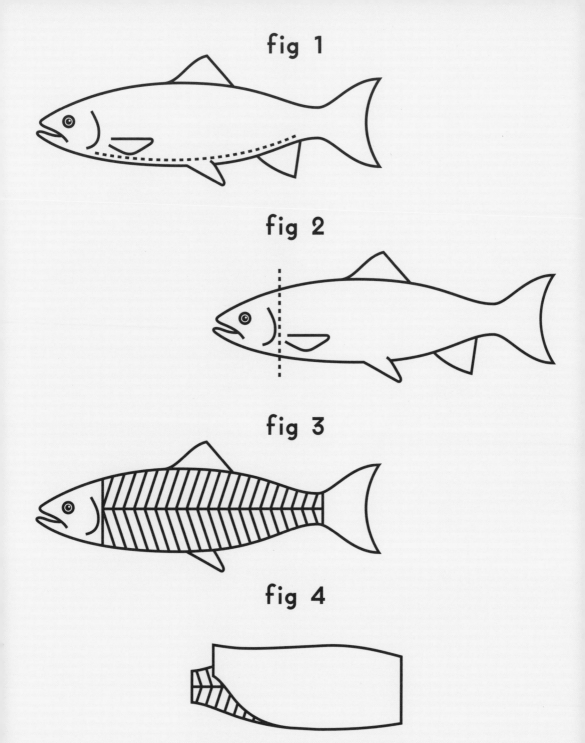

fig 1

fig 2

fig 3

fig 4

23

Perfectly cooked, tender grains of rice are an ideal base for any poke bowl. While rice cookers offer an easy and reliable route to fluffy rice heaven, hob cooking is easy enough to master. We use white, brown or black short-grain rice in our recipes. Cooking techniques vary for each, so follow the steps below carefully, depending on the grain you have selected.

The following method will yield approximately 480 g (1 lb 1 oz/2½ cups) cooked rice.

Cooking Rice

Step 1

Weigh out 240 g (8½ oz/1 cup) rice and place in a saucepan with a close-fitting lid.

Step 2

Rinse! Cover the rice with cold water and, using your hand, stir gently to release the excess starch from the grains. Drain and repeat until the water stops turning cloudy.

Step 3

Once fully rinsed and drained, cover the rice with the following amount of cold water:

White rice .... 240 ml (8 fl oz/1 cup)
Brown rice .... 360 ml (12 fl oz/1½ cups)
Black rice .... 480 ml (16 fl oz/2 cups)
(soak black rice for up to 1 hour before cooking)

Step 4

Place the saucepan on a medium-high heat and bring to a rapid boil. Cover, turn down the heat to a gentle simmer, and cook for the following length of time:

White rice ....15–20 minutes
Brown rice .... 20 minutes
Black rice ....30 minutes

Step 5

Once the rice is cooked, remove the pan from the heat and leave, covered, to steam for a further 10 minutes.

Step 6

Now you can turn the rice out into a wooden sushi rice bowl, if you have one. Using a rice paddle or wooden spoon, gently fold and turn the cooked rice, allowing the steam to evaporate.

Step 7

At this stage, we like to season the freshly cooked rice. Whisk together 2 tablespoons of mirin with 2 tablespoons of rice wine vinegar, plus 1 teaspoon of sugar and ½ a teaspoon of salt. Drizzle the mixture over the hot rice while gently folding to coat each grain.

Step 8

The rice should now be left for 10 minutes to cool before using for your poke bowl.

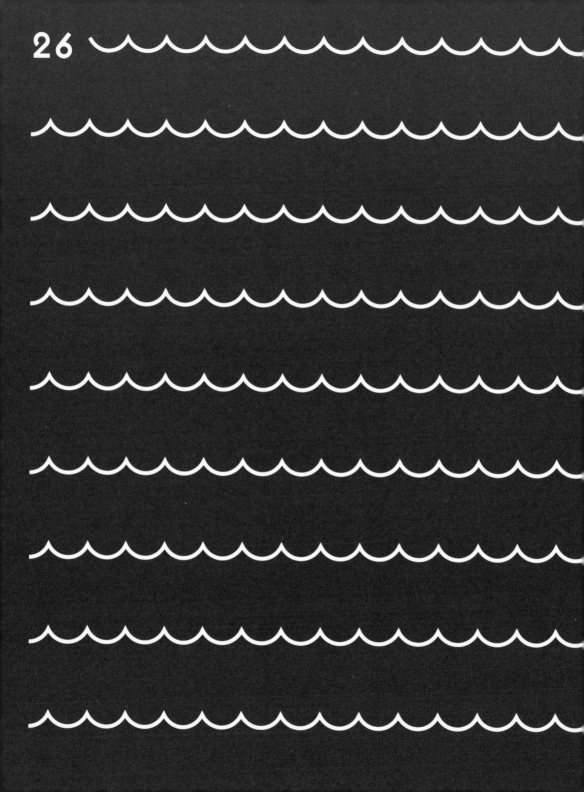

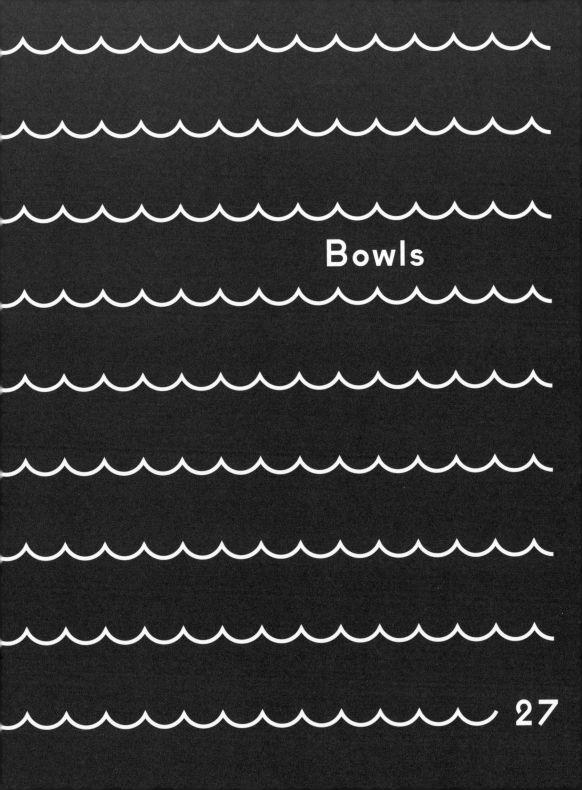

Bowls

Tuna

Ahi Poke Hawaiian Style

Serves 4

Pimp it!

Beetroot Pickled
Baby Corn
(page 73)

—

Lotus Root Crisps
(page 110)

—

edible violet flowers

Base

- 240 g (8½ oz/1½ cups) white sushi rice

Poke

- 400 g (14 oz) fresh yellowfin tuna, cut into 1.5 cm (½ inch) cubes
- 2 tbsp sliced Maui or sweet white onion
- 4 tbsp spring onions (scallions), just the green tops, finely sliced
- ½ tsp toasted white sesame seeds
- ½ tsp toasted black sesame seeds
- 1 tsp alaea or Hawaiian sea salt (sea salt or Himalayan salt are good alternatives)

Marinade

- 4 tsp toasted sesame oil
- 2 tbsp tamari soy sauce
- 1 tsp grated fresh ginger
- 1 tsp black sesame seeds, lightly toasted
- 1 tsp white sesame seeds, lightly toasted
- pinch of sugar

Our homage to a contemporary Hawaiian-style poke, traditionally served with limu kohu (seaweed) and Hawaiian salt. We've tried to create a similar version with variations on these classic ingredients. Hopefully the taste will transport you to the islands!

Cook the rice as per the cooking instructions (page 25) and leave to cool.

In a large mixing bowl combine the tuna, white onion, half of the spring onions, half of the black and white sesame seeds, and the salt.

Mix all the marinade ingredients together in a small bowl, add to the tuna and thoroughly combine. Serve immediately or leave to marinate for up to 1 hour.

Once ready to serve, spoon the cooked rice into 4 bowls and top with the fish and marinade.

Sprinkle the remaining sesame seeds and spring onions loosely over the top of the dish. Try pimping your bowls with Beetroot Pickled Baby Corn, Lotus Root Crisps and a few edible violet flowers.

Ahi Poke with Gochujang Broccoli Salad

Serves 4

Pimp it!

Pickled Cucumber
(page 68)

Poke

— 240 g (8½ oz) fresh yellowfin tuna, cut into 1.5 cm (½ inch) cubes
— 2½ tbsp Shoyu Marinade (page 81)
— 2 spring onions (scallions), finely sliced
— 1 tbsp toasted white sesame seeds

Salad

— 1 large head of broccoli, thinly sliced with a mandoline
— 1 firm red tomato, quartered, deseeded and finely diced
— 1 small bunch of fresh chives, finely chopped
— Nori Furikake (page 93)

Dressing

— 2 tbsp gochujang paste
— 1 tbsp sugar
— 2 tbsp rice wine vinegar
— 1 tbsp olive oil
— 1 tbsp sesame oil
— 2 tbsp soy sauce
— 1 garlic clove, peeled and crushed
— 1 lime, freshly squeezed

Gochujang paste is the base of many a great kimchi recipes. Here it adds a spicy kick to the crunchy, raw broccoli salad with no fermenting required!

Lightly coat the tuna in the shoyu marinade and add the spring onions. Cover and leave in the fridge while you prepare the salad ingredients.

Place the broccoli, tomato and chives in a large bowl.

Whisk together the dressing ingredients in a small bowl or jar. Just before serving, pour the dressing over the salad and toss lightly.

Divide the salad between 4 bowls and top with the tuna poke, Nori Furikake and toasted sesame seeds.

Base

- 240 g (8½ oz/1¼ cups) white sushi rice
- 100 g (3½ oz/½ cup) tinned black beans (drained weight), rinsed
- ½ bunch coriander (cilantro), roughly chopped

Garnish

- 2 sweetcorn cobs, husks removed
- 2 tsp groundnut oil (or other light flavourless oil)
- 1 red onion, thinly sliced
- pinch of salt
- squeeze of lemon
- 1 lime, cut into quarters

Poke

- 400 g (14 oz) fresh yellowfin tuna, cut into 1.5 cm (½ inch) cubes

Marinade

- 3 tbsp mayonnaise
- 1 tsp liquid smoke
- ½ lemon, freshly squeezed

Mexican Ahi in with Sweetcorn Smoky Mayo

Serves 4

Our slightly more sophisticated take on a classic tuna and sweetcorn combination. The smoky mayo is really addictive, so be careful. Liquid smoke is a cheat, but you will add it to everything once you have it in the cupboard.

Preheat the oven to 200°C (400°F/Gas 6).

Cook the sushi rice as per the cooking instructions (page 25) and leave to cool. Once cool, Add the black beans and coriander, mix and set aside.

For the garnish, coat the corn in a little oil and then cook in the oven for 20 minutes. Once the corn is cool enough, char it on the flame of the hob. Once blackened, hold the corn cobs vertically on a chopping board and carefully remove the kernels using a sharp knife.

Soak the red onion in water with a squeeze of lemon and a pinch of salt for 15 minutes.

Combine the tuna with the marinade ingredients.

Assemble the dish, starting with the rice and bean mix, then the marinated tuna and the corn. Drain and dry the red onion and place on top. Serve each bowl with a wedge of lime and green chilli.

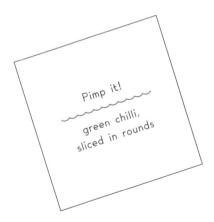

Pimp it!

green chilli, sliced in rounds

Tropical Ahi Poke

Serves 4

Pimp it!

finely diced papaya
for an extra fruity hit

—

roasted cashew nuts
for crunch

—

edible flowers

Base

— 240 g (8½ oz/1¼ cups) short-grain black rice

Marinade

— 125 ml (4 fl oz/½ cup) tinned full-fat coconut milk
— 3 tbsp tamari or light soy sauce
— 2 tsp sesame oil
— 1 tsp finely chopped fresh ginger
— squeeze of lime juice
— pinch of salt
— 1 tsp sesame seeds

Poke

— 400 g (14 oz) fresh yellowfin tuna, cut into 1.5 cm (½ inch) cubes (albacore would also work well)
— ½ tsp toasted black sesame seeds
— ½ tsp toasted white sesame seeds

Salad

— ¼ pineapple, julienned
— 1 mango, julienned
— 1 red (bell) pepper, finely diced (optional)
— 4 mm (⅛ inch) piece of fresh ginger, julienned
— 1 red chilli, deseeded and sliced into rounds
— couple of fresh coriander (cilantro) leaves, thinly sliced
— 1 tsp freshly squeezed lime juice
— pinch of salt
— ¼ avocado, sliced

This bowl of tropical vibes is fresh and fun. The sweet fruit works beautifully with the tuna in the coconut marinade, coming together to celebrate the Pacific and South Pacific islands in all their tropical glory. This dish does not disappoint.

Cook the rice as per the cooking instructions (page 25) and leave to cool.

Prepare the marinade by adding all the ingredients to a bowl and mixing well. If the consistency is too thick, add a little water. Coat the fish in the marinade and set aside.

In a large mixing bowl, combine the pineapple, mango, red pepper (if using), ginger, chilli, coriander, lime juice, salt and mix together.

When ready to serve, divide the rice among the bowls, fan out the avocado and add the salad, then spoon the marinated fish on top of the rice. Sprinkle a few sesame seeds loosely over the top of the dish.

Spicy Ahi Poke with Wontons + Mango Salsa

Serves 4

This is a great sharing dish, so it's ideal for a party or gathering. Place bowls of fried wontons, spicy tuna poke and salsa in the middle of the table and let everybody dig in.

Quick Pickled Onions

- 1 large Maui or sweet white onion, sliced into thin rounds
- 75 ml (2½ fl oz/⅓ cup) rice wine vinegar
- 3 tbsp sugar
- pinch of sea salt

Salsa

- 2 red tomatoes, deseeded and finely chopped
- 1 red (bell) pepper, deseeded and finely chopped
- 1 avocado, diced
- ½ mango, diced
- juice of 1 lime

Poke

- 360 g (13 oz) fresh yellowfin tuna, cut into 1.5 cm (½ inch) cubes
- 4 tbsp Spicy Marinade (page 79)

Wontons

- 2 litres (68 fl oz/8 cups) vegetable oil, for frying
- 24 wonton wrappers, cut in half on the diagonal

Begin by making the quick pickled onions. Place the sliced onion in a bowl. Combine the vinegar, sugar and salt and pour over the onion. Set to one side and allow to marinate for at least 30 minutes.

Next, gently mix together all the ingredients for the salsa in a bowl, season with salt, cover and leave in the fridge until ready to serve.

In a bowl, dress the cubes of tuna in the Spicy Marinade and refrigerate for 1 hour.

To fry the wontons, heat the oil in a saucepan to around 180°C (350°F). Drop the wonton wrappers into the oil in batches, taking care not to overcrowd the pan. They should sizzle and puff up. Remove with a slotted spoon once golden brown and drain on paper towels. Although best freshly fried, wonton wrappers should keep crisp for up to 24 hours in an airtight container.

Serve the wontons topped with the spicy poke, pickled onions and salsa. Try pimping with a drizzle of Spicy Mayo, Nori Furikake and a sprinkling of amaranth micro herbs.

Pimp it!

Spicy Mayo
(page 80)
—
Nori Furikake
(page 93)
—
amaranth micro herbs

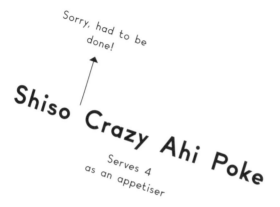

Pimp it!

extra shiso leaves as a
garnish

—

toasted macadamia
add crunch and richness
to the dish

Sorry, had to be
done!

Shiso Crazy Ahi Poke

Serves 4
as an appetiser

Poke

— 2 spring onions (scallions), white and green
  ends, finely sliced
— 2 tbsp sesame oil or Shiso Oil (page 83)
— 400 g (14 oz) fresh yellowfin tuna, cut into
  1.5 cm (½ inch) cubes
— 8 fresh shiso leaves (basil leaves could
  also work)
— 10 g (4 oz) hijiki seaweed (dehydrated
  weight), rehydrated
— pinch of alaea or Hawaiian sea salt
  (sea salt or Himalayan are good alternatives)

This is a punchy little starter with real
presence due to the shiso. The shiso leaf has
a basil and anise flavour, and we go crazy
for it. It tastes and looks beautiful and
always gets people talking. To make this into
a main dish, simply double the quantities given
here and add to our purple rice, which is a
combination of white and black rice (page 25).

Add the spring onion to a mixing bowl, along
with the sesame or shiso oil and tuna. Tightly
roll up the shiso leaves, two at a time, thinly
slice and add to the tuna. Add the hijiki and
mix everything together, then season with salt.

Scallops with Chicory + Lemongrass

Serves 4
as an appetiser or side

Chicory

— 1 white chicory (Belgian endive), leaves separated
— 1 tsp olive oil
— 1 tsp salt

Spicy Pineapple Relish

— 50 g (2 oz) pineapple flesh, diced into 3 mm (⅛ inch) cubes
— ¼ bird's eye chilli, minced
— 3 fresh mint leaves, finely shredded
— 1 tbsp olive oil
— squeeze of lemon juice

Scallops

— 4 fresh scallops, cleaned, roe removed and diced in to 3 mm (⅛ inch) cubes
— Lemongrass and Kaffir Lime Leaf Oil
(page 83)

Scallops are delicious served raw, especially when dressed with delicately fragranced lemongrass oil. This makes an impressive starter, while the pineapple relish on its own can be used to spice up plenty of other vegetarian and fish dishes.

Preheat the oven to 180°C (350°F/Gas 4).

Begin by roasting the chicory leaves for 10 minutes. Once roasted, remove from the oven and rub with a little oil and salt and dice into 3 mm (⅛ inch) cubes. Set aside.

For the pineapple relish, mix together all the ingredients in a bowl, then keep in the fridge until ready to serve. This will keep for up to 3 days.

When ready to serve, mix the roasted chicory and the scallops in a bowl and season with salt. Put a small pile on a plate and drizzle over the oil. Serve with the spicy pineapple relish.

Spicy Tobiko Salmon

Serves 4

Base

— 240 g (8½ oz/1 cup) short-grain brown rice

Salad

— 3 carrots, peeled
— 2 baby cucumbers
— 125 ml (4 fl oz/½ cup) tamari soy sauce
— 60 ml (2 fl oz/¼ cup) dashi stock
— 60 g (2 oz/¼ cup) sugar
— 125 ml (4 fl oz/½ cup) rice wine vinegar

Poke

— 2 large fresh salmon fillets (approx.
400 g/14 oz), skin removed and cut into
1.5 cm (½ inch) cubes

Marinade

— 75 g (3 oz/⅓ cup) Spicy Mayo (page 80)
— ½ tbsp tobiko (flying fish roe)
— 2 tsp yuzu kosho chilli paste (this is fiery
stuff, so add bit by bit until desired level
of spiciness is achieved)

Garnish

— 2 green chillis, thinly sliced
— 2 tbsp Nori Furikake (page 93)

The bright orange tobiko adds a delicately smoky flavour and an interesting, crunchy texture. Piled onto the salmon, it also lends an impressive volcanic appearance to this fiery dish.

Cook the rice as per the cooking instructions (page 25) and leave to cool.

Use a julienne peeler to create long, thin strips from the carrots and cucumbers and transfer to a bowl. Whisk together the remaining ingredients to make a dressing then pour over the salad.

Gently fold the salmon poke into the marinade ingredients and thoroughly coat.

To assemble, start with a base of the brown rice, top with the salad and pile the fish on top. Garnish with green chillies and furikake. Try pimping with extra tobiko and a side of Pickled Cucumbers.

Pimp it!

extra tobiko
—
Pickled Cucumber
(page 68)

Wasabi Salmon Poke with Goma Wakame

Serves 4

Base

— 240 g (8½ oz/1¼ cups) short-grain black rice

Wasabi and Coriander Mayo

— big handful of fresh coriander (cilantro) leaves, finely chopped
— 120 g (4 oz) Basic Japanese Mayo (page 80)
— 1 lime, freshly squeezed
— 15 g (½ oz) prepared wasabi paste
— 10 g (¼ oz) fresh ginger, finely chopped

Goma Seaweed Salad

— 60 g (2 oz) dried wakame, rehydrated in cold water for 5 minutes
— 40 g (1½ oz) goma seaweed salad (a pre-marinated seaweed, found frozen in most Japanese or Vietnamese stores)
— 1 spring onion (scallion), finely sliced
— 2 Soy Pickled Shiitake, diced (page 69), plus 100 ml (3½ fl oz/½ cup) of the pickling liquor

Poke

— 4–6 tbsp Shoyu Marinade (page 79)
— 2 tsp sesame seeds, toasted
— 2 large fresh salmon fillets, approx. 400 g (14 oz), skinned and cut into 1.5 cm (½ inch) cubes
— 2 tbsp wasabi peas, crushed

Pimp it!

Soy-Pickled Shiitake
(page 69)
—
coriander cress
(micro cilantro)

We love the spicy kick of wasabi, especially in crunchy wasabi peas scattered over poke.

Cook the rice as per the cooking instructions (page 25), leave to cool and set aside.

Next, make the wasabi and coriander mayo. Blitz half of the coriander with the rest of ingredients in a food processor. Add the rest of the coriander and pulse until smooth. Set aside.

For the salad, combine all the ingredients in a bowl and set aside.

To make the salmon poke, toss the Shoyu Marinade, sesame seeds and salmon together in a bowl. Pile the poke in bowls on top of the rice and seaweed salad. Drizzle over the wasabi and coriander mayo, and sprinkle over some crushed wasabi peas. Try pimping with extra pickled shiitake and a sprinkling of coriander.

Lomi Lomi Salmon

Serves 2
as an appetiser

Pimp it!

crushed ice

—

garnish with finely sliced
spring onion (scallions)

This refreshing dish celebrates the versatility of a wonderful fish – the salmon. This dish was supposedly introduced to Hawaii by visiting sailors. Traditionally served ice-cold, it should ideally be served on ice or straight from the fridge.

Cured Salmon

If you can't buy pre-salted salmon, you can cure it yourself at home – it is super-easy!

— 100 g (3½ oz / ⅓ cup) sea salt (the larger the salt granules, the better)
— 100 g (3½ oz / ⅓ cup) smoked sea salt
— 100 g (3½ oz / ½ cup) soft brown sugar
— 500 g (1 lb 2 oz) fresh salmon, pin boned and skin removed (you can always ask your fishmonger to help)

Salad

— 6 medium heritage tomatoes (if not available any sweet tomato will work)
— 100 g (3½ oz / ⅔ cup) sliced Maui or sweet white onion

Marinade

— 1 tsp toasted sesame oil
— 1 tsp grated fresh ginger
— pinch of sugar
— squeeze of lime juice

If curing the salmon, place a piece of cling film (plastic wrap), about 30 cm (12 inches) square, on the work surface. Mix together the salts and sugar, scatter half on the cling film and lay the salmon on top. Use the remaining cure mix to cover the fish. Wrap the salmon tightly in the cling film and leave in the fridge for 12–24 hours. The longer you leave it, the firmer it will become.

Rinse the salt cure from the salmon. We recommend tasting the fish to determine the flavour – if too salty, you can soak the fillet in water for up to 1 hour. Just remember this dish is flavoured by the saltiness of the fish. Once happy, cut into 4 mm (⅛ inch) cubes and add to a mixing bowl.

Prepare the salad by cutting the tomatoes into cubes about the same size as the fish, removing the seeds. Do the same with the sweet white onion. Add to the fish, along with the marinade ingredients. This can be served straight away or left to marinate for up to an hour. The key is to keep it ice-cold. For real wow factor, serve on crushed ice with a scattering of sliced spring onions.

Salmon Poke with Ponzu Kale

Serves 4

Base

— 240 g (8½ oz/1¼ cups) short-grain black rice

Poke

— 300 g (10½ oz) fresh salmon, cut into
  1 cm (½ inch) cubes
— 3 tbsp Shoyu Marinade (page 79)

Salad

— 4 generous handfuls of kale, tough stems
  removed, leaves torn
— drizzle of light olive oil
— 2 tbsp roughly chopped fresh coriander
  (cilantro) leaves
— 60 g (2 oz/1 cup) shelled edamame
  beans, (cooked according to the packet
  instructions)
— 2 tsp toasted white sesame seeds

Ponzu Dressing (will make more then needed)

— 120 ml (4 fl oz/½ cup) tamari soy sauce
— 60 ml (2 fl oz/¼ cup) rice wine vinegar
— juice of 1 lemon
— juice of ½ orange
— 1 tsp bottled yuzu juice

Garnish

— 1 tbsp chopped toasted macadamia nuts
— spring onions (scallions), finely sliced
— Nori Furikake (page 93)

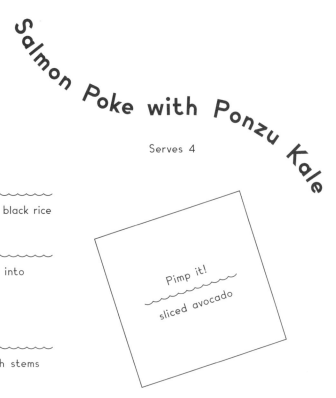

Pimp it!

sliced avocado

**We love a citrus marinade for oilier fish such
as salmon. This ponzu kale was one of the
first recipes we trialled on the markets and it
quickly became a favourite.**

Cook the rice as per the cooking instructions
(page 25) and leave to cool.
   Toss the fish in the Shoyu Marinade to
lightly coat. Taste and adjust the seasoning
if necessary.
   For the salad, massage the kale with a
little oil until tender, then toss with the
coriander, edamame and sesame seeds.
   Mix together the ponzu dressing ingredients
and spoon over the salad.
   Pile the rice into 4 bowls, then top with the
kale and fish. Sprinkle with the toasted nuts,
spring onions and furikake.

Pimp it!

tamari soy sauce

Pickled Quail's Eggs

- 250 ml (8 fl oz/1 cup) boiled water
- 125 ml (4 fl oz/½ cup) rice wine vinegar
- 3 tbsp sugar
- 2 tsp salt
- 1 raw beetroot (beet), peeled and roughly sliced
- 12 quail's eggs

Base

- 240 g (8½ oz/1 cup) short-grain brown rice

Poke

- 300 g (10½ oz) cold smoked salmon, skin removed if necessary, cut into 1 cm (½ inch) cubes

Garnish

- 1 avocado, sliced
- kizami nori (shredded nori)
- 1 lemon, cut into wedges
- few sprigs of coriander cress (micro cilantro)
- black and white sesame seeds

This dish was our answer to creating a poke brunch dish when we first began trading with Kerb. Our initial starting point was a Hawaiian take on kedgeree. All the elements of our classic salmon bowl are here, but we swap out fresh salmon for smoked. The pink pickled quail's eggs are fiddly but worth it.

Begin by making the pickling liquor for the quail's eggs. Combine the water, vinegar, sugar and salt in a pan and bring to a simmer over a medium heat. Add the beetroot and cook for 10 minutes before removing from the heat and allowing to cool fully.

Next, soft-boil the quail's eggs. Bring a pan of water to the boil, gently place in the eggs and boil for 2 minutes. Drain the eggs and put them into a bowl of ice water to stop them overcooking. Once cooled, carefully peel off the shells and add to the cooled beetroot pickling liquor. Leave to pickle for 30 minutes, at which point the eggs will be dyed a deep pink.

Cook the rice as per the cooking instructions (page 25) and leave to cool.

Assemble the dish by dividing the rice among the bowls and topping with the smoked salmon, sliced avocado and kizami nori. Slice the quail's eggs in half and place yolk side up in the bowls. Finish with a slice of lemon, sprinkle with coriander cress and sesame seeds. Try pimping with a drizzle of tamari soy sauce.

Smoked Salmon Poke with Avocado + Pink Pickled Egg

Serves 4

Mackerel Poke with Ginger + Chive Pesto

Serves 4

Pimp it!

a few sprigs of coriander cress (micro cilantro)

–

Pickled Cucumbers

(page 68)

–

edible flowers

Pickles

- 60 ml (2 fl oz / ¼ cup) rice wine vinegar
- 2 tbsp sugar
- pinch of sea salt flakes
- 1 bunch of radishes, stalks and leaves removed, finely sliced

Base

- 240 g (8½ oz / 1 cup) short-grain brown rice

Pesto

- 4 tbsp finely crushed fresh ginger
- 2 tbsp rice wine vinegar
- 3 tbsp mirin
- 4 tbsp thinly sliced fresh chives
- 10 g (½ oz / ¼ cup) finely chopped fresh coriander (cilantro) leaves
- pinch of sea salt flakes

Poke

- 4 fresh mackerel fillets, cut down the middle to remove the line of thin, spiny bones
- 2 tsp toasted sesame oil

The spicy ginger and chive pesto cuts through the rich, oily mackerel a treat here. This pesto would work equally well with other oily fish and also stirred through cooked grains or popped on top of fatty pork belly.

Begin by making the pickles. Combine the vinegar, sugar and salt and stir until the sugar dissolves. Add the radish. Refrigerate for at least 30 minutes.

Cook the rice as per the cooking instructions (page 25), set aside and leave to cool.

For the pesto, sweat the ginger in a saucepan over a low heat with the vinegar and mirin for 25–30 minutes (until the liquid has mostly evaporated). Cool. Stir through the chives and coriander and season with the salt.

Take the mackerel and carefully remove the thin, tough membrane that covers the patterned skin, then slice the fish into 1.5 cm (½ inch) cubes. Combine with the sesame oil.

To assemble, spoon the cooled rice into bowls and place the mackerel poke on top with the pesto and pickled radishes. Try pimping with coriander cress, Pickled Cucumbers and garnish with an edible flower.

Poke

〜〜〜〜〜〜〜〜〜〜〜〜〜〜〜〜〜〜〜〜〜

— 4 fresh mackerel fillets, cut down the middle
to remove the line of thin, spiny bones

Pickling Liquor

〜〜〜〜〜〜〜〜〜〜〜〜〜〜〜〜〜〜〜〜〜

— 700 ml (24 fl oz/3 cups) rice wine vinegar
— 150 ml (5 fl oz/⅔ cup) mirin
— 1 tbsp sugar
— 1 tbsp sea salt

Horseradish Cream

〜〜〜〜〜〜〜〜〜〜〜〜〜〜〜〜〜〜〜〜〜

— 30 g (1 oz/⅓ cup) peeled and finely
grated fresh horseradish root
— 150 g (5½ oz/⅔ cup) sour cream
— 150 g (5½ oz/⅔ cup) full-fat
Greek-style yoghurt
— small pinch of Japanese mustard
powder (optional)
— squeeze of lemon juice
— salt and freshly ground black pepper

Rye Crumbs

〜〜〜〜〜〜〜〜〜〜〜〜〜〜〜〜〜〜〜〜〜

— 1 tbsp butter
— 2 slices of German-style dark rye bread,
pulsed to breadcrumbs in a food processor

Salad

〜〜〜〜〜〜〜〜〜〜〜〜〜〜〜〜〜〜〜〜〜

— 3 raw beetroot (beets) (try to get a mix
of red and candy), peeled and julienned
— ½ mooli (daikon), peeled and julienned
— a few sprigs of amaranth micro herbs

Pickled Mackerel, Mooli + Beetroot Salad with Rye Crumbs

Serves 4

**This is a poke take on the classic Nordic
combination of rye, beetroot (beet) and fish.
The pickled mackerel adds tang, while toasting
the rye breadcrumbs provide a crunchy texture
and releases its nutty aroma.**

Place the mackerel fillets skin side up in a dish
without overlapping. Combine the pickling liquor
ingredients together and pour over the mackerel.
Leave in the fridge to marinate for 1 hour.

Make the horseradish cream by stirring
the horseradish into the sour cream and yoghurt
and seasoning well with mustard powder (if
using), lemon juice, salt and pepper.

Next, melt the butter for the rye crumbs
in a frying pan (skillet) over medium-high heat.
Toss in the rye breadcrumbs and continue to
move around the pan until the crumbs are
browned and toasted.

Remove the mackerel fillets from the pickling
liquor and place skin side up on a board
Carefully remove the thin, tough membrane
that covers the patterned skin, then slice the
fish into 1.5 cm (½ inch) pieces.

To serve, place a small pile of beetroot
and mooli on a plate, place the pickled mackerel
poke alongside, then add a dollop of horseradish
cream and a generous sprinkle of the crunchy
rye crumbs. Garnish with amaranth micro herbs.

Sea Bass Ceviche with Green Papaya Slaw

Dressing

- juice of 10 limes
- 4 tbsp finely chopped fresh ginger
- 2 garlic cloves, peeled and crushed
- 6 tbsp fish sauce
- 2 tbsp soft brown sugar
- 2 mild red chillies, finely diced

Slaw

- 240 g (8½ oz) green mango, julienned
- 360 g (13 oz) green papaya, julienned
- 160 g (5½ oz) carrots, julienned
- 360 g (13 oz) heritage tomatoes, deseeded and cut into eighths
- 2 large handfuls fresh coriander (cilantro) leaves and stems, finely chopped

Marinade

- 120 ml (4 fl oz/½ cup) tinned full-fat coconut milk
- 140 ml (5 fl oz/⅔ cup) freshly squeezed lime juice
- 60 ml (2 fl oz/¼ cup) cold water
- 1 mild red chilli, finely diced
- 1 tsp sea salt

Ceviche

- 2 large fresh sea bass, filleted, pin boned and skin removed, cut into 1 cm (½ inch) cubes

Pimp it!

roasted cashew nuts, chopped

–

Crispy Onion Furikake
(page 93)

The classic Thai green papaya salad, som tam, perfectly balances sweet, salty and sour flavours with an underbelly of spice from the red chillies. Here, we have topped it with a sea bass ceviche lightly cured in lime and coconut milk for extra tropical zing.

Whisk together all the ingredients for the dressing until the sugar has dissolved. Toss with the prepared vegetables for the slaw and set to one side.

To make the marinade, combine the coconut milk, lime juice and water, in a separate bowl. Add the sea bass cubes and mix in, along with the chilli and salt. Allow to marinate for 5 minutes.

To serve, divide the slaw among 4 bowls, then top with the sea bass ceviche.

Sour Sea Bass with Grapefruit, Mint + Baby Watercress in a Ponzu Dressing

Serves 2 as an appetiser

Grapefruit Ponzu Dressing

- 1½ tbsp grapefruit juice
- 1½ tbsp lemon juice
- 2 tbsp mirin
- 5 tbsp soy sauce
- 1 tbsp sugar
- 2 tbsp rice wine vinegar

Poke

- ½ pink grapefruit, cut into segments, pith removed
- few fresh mint leaves
- small handful of baby watercress (the baby watercress has a milder flavour)
- 160 g (5½ oz) fresh sea bass fillets, pin boned and skin removed, cut into 1.5 cm (½ inch) cubes
- black sesame seeds

We love a ponzu dressing! It is vibrant, fresh, tangy and really brings a dish alive. It is also a great alternative to an oil-based marinade. This summery dish works well to get the palate fired up for a dinner. We've used sea bass, but any other meaty white fish would also work.

Make the dressing in advance: combine all the ingredients together in a bowl and leave to infuse. Alternatively, combine the ingredients together in a saucepan and bring to the boil. Remove from the heat and leave to cool. Once cool, pour into a sealable jar and keep in the fridge. It should last for at least 1 week.

In a bowl, combine the grapefruit, mint leaves and baby watercress with the dressing. Give it a quick stir and transfer to a serving plate. Add the sea bass and sprinkle a few black sesame seeds over the top, to garnish.

Marinade (Tiger's Milk)

- juice of 8 limes
- juice of ½ orange
- 2 tbsp cold water
- ½ mild red chilli, finely diced
- ½ tsp sea salt
- 4 mm (⅛ inch) piece of fresh ginger, julienned
- couple of fresh coriander (cilantro) stalks, finely chopped

Base

- 300 g (10½ oz/1½ cups) black quinoa
- 2 handfuls fresh coriander (cilantro) leaves and stems, finely chopped

Salad

- 1 red onion, peeled and finely sliced
- 2 pears, julienned
- 1 kohlrabi, julienned

Ceviche

- 10 large fresh tiger prawns (shrimp) (ask your fishmonger to get the freshest possible)

Pimp it!

for texture add some salted corn to the dish

Ceviche King Prawn with Kohlrabi, Pear + Black Quinoa

Serves 4

This tangy, fresh, summery dish is a lovely way to eat prawns (shrimp). It is important to get them as fresh as possible from your fishmonger. For the ceviche, we marinate the fish in a citrus-based, spicy Peruvian marinade called tiger's milk – this stuff is so good you could drink it!

Combine all the ingredients for the tiger's milk in a bowl, and let them infuse for 4 hours.

Rinse the quinoa in cold water. Transfer to a pan, cover with water and bring to the boil. Reduce the heat and simmer for 15 minutes. The grains will swell but should still have a little bite. Once cooked, drain well and place in a bowl to cool and dry.

For the salad, soak the red onion in water for 15 minutes. Drain and dry the onion, then combine with the pear and kohlrabi.

Rinse the prawns under cold water, peel and cut off the heads. De-vein by making a small incision along the back and removing the vein. Lightly salt the prawns, then place in the marinade to cure/cook in the acidity of the lime juice. This should take about 10 minutes.

To serve, lightly season the quinoa with salt and a teaspoon of the tiger's milk, then stir through the coriander. Pile up the salad and prawns, then spoon over some more of the tiger's milk, and enjoy!

Boiling Liquor

- 6 tbsp rice wine vinegar
- 4 tbsp tamari soy sauce
- 1 litre (35 fl oz) water
- 1 tsp salt
- 2 garlic cloves, peeled

Poke

- 1 kg (2 lb 4 oz) defrosted octopus – ideally a double sucker (the freezing and thawing process helps tenderise the flesh)
- 200 g (7 oz) kimchi (store-bought)
- 2 tbsp sliced Maui or sweet white onion

Base

- 240 g (8½ oz/1¼ cups) white sushi rice

Marinade

- 300 g (10 ½ oz) kimchi, (store-bought) blitzed into a sauce
- juice of ½ orange
- 2 tsp toasted sesame oil
- ½ tsp smoked paprika
- generous pinch of sugar

Pimp it!

spring onions
(scallions)
–
black sesame seeds

Octopus

Tako Kimchi Poke

Serves 4

This is a must! If cooked properly, octopus, or tako as it is called on the islands, is so dope! With a little prep and patience, this dish never disappoints. The kimchi marinade adds a really lovely deep flavour and the charring helps to bring out the summer vibes.

To cook the octopus, place all the ingredients for the boiling liquor in a large pan and bring to the boil. Just before dropping the octopus into the water, curl the tentacles by dipping them into the water for a few seconds and lifting them out again. Repeat this 3 times. Then submerge the octopus completely and simmer for 1¾ hours.

Lift the octopus out of the water and set to one side to cool. Remove the tentacles and place in a bowl with the kimchi and leave to marinate for at least 2 hours.

Cook the rice as per the cooking instructions (page 25) and leave to cool.

For the marinade, blitz together all the ingredients with a touch of water to help loosen the mix.

Now for the charring. Heat up the BBQ or grill, and once it's super-hot, add the octopus tentacles and onion. While they are cooking, baste with half of the marinade. You are looking for a quick char, so just a couple of minutes on each side should do it.

Cut the octopus into 1.5 cm (½ inch) discs. Add the onions and pile on top of the cooled rice. Stack some of the kimchi from the poke on the side, then pour over the remaining marinade and let it soak into the rice.

Pimp it!
~~~~~~~~
Pineapple Kimchi
(page 74)

Spicy Tempeh Poke with Beetroot + Quinoa Salad

Fermented soybeans →

Serves 4

Poke

— 350 g (12 oz) tempeh, cut into 2 cm (¾ inch) cubes
— 2 tsp garlic powder
— 2 tsp onion powder
— 2 tsp paprika
— 2 tsp chilli powder
— zest of 2 lemons

Salad

— 100 g (3½ oz / ½ cup) quinoa
— 2 beetroot (beets), cooked and cut into 1 cm (½ inch) cubes
— 100 g (3½ oz / ⅓ cup) tinned chickpeas (garbanzo beans), drained and rinsed
— 2 handfuls of spinach, torn
— 2 carrots, peeled and julienned
— 2 tsp white sesame seeds, toasted
— 2 roasted red (bell) peppers, cut into 5 mm (¼ inch) cubes

Dressing

— 1 tbsp Tabasco (hot pepper sauce)
— 200 ml (7 fl oz / ¾ cup) olive oil
— juice of 2 limes
— 2 tsp mirin
— 2 tsp soy sauce
— 2 garlic cloves, peeled and crushed
— 2 shallots, finely chopped

This vegan poke is such a colourful and vibrant dish, full of fresh vegetables and subtle spice and packed with protein.

Preheat the oven to 180°C (350°F/Gas 4).

For the poke, toss together the tempeh, spices and lemon zest. Arrange the coated tempeh on a lightly oiled baking tray and roast in the oven for 20 minutes.

To make the salad, rinse the quinoa in cold water. Transfer to a saucepan, cover with water and bring to the boil. Reduce the heat and simmer for 15 minutes. The grains will swell but should still have a little bite. Once cooked, drain well and place in a bowl to cool. Add the remaining salad ingredients to the quinoa.

Whisk together the dressing ingredients and pour over the salad. Toss gently to combine.

To serve, divide the salad among 4 plates and scatter the roasted tempeh over the top.

Pimp it!

Beetroot Pickled
Baby Corn
(page 73)

—

Pickled Cucumbers
(page 68)

—

fresh enoki mushrooms

—

spring onions (scallions),
finely sliced

Tofu + Shiitake Poke

Serves 4

Base

— 240 g (8½ oz/1¼ cups) short-grain black rice

Poke

— 500 g (1 lb 2 oz) firm, fresh tofu
— 400 g (14 oz) Soy Pickled Shiitake (page 69)
— 100 ml (3½ fl oz/½ cup) Sweet Miso Sauce (page 89)
— 2 tbsp Nori Furikake (page 93)

Salad

— 3 carrots, julienned
— 100 g (3½ oz) radishes, thinly sliced with a mandoline
— 50 g (2 oz/¾ cup) shelled edamame beans, cooked as per the instructions on the packet
— 5 g (¼ oz) dried wakame, rehydrated in cold water for 5 minutes

This is our hero veggie dish. Tofu is a great flavour vehicle and we partner it here with a sweet miso dressing and tangy soy pickled shiitake.

Cook the rice as per the cooking instructions (page 25) and leave to cool.

Drain the tofu, pat dry using paper towels. and slice into 1.5 cm (½ inch) cubes. Set aside.

Slice the pickled shiitake, removing the stalks and set aside.

In a bowl, combine all the salad ingredients.

To serve, divide the rice among 4 bowls. Top with the cubed tofu, shiitake, a generous drizzle of miso dressing and furikake. Serve with the salad. Try pimping with extra pickles, fresh enoki mushrooms and spring onions.

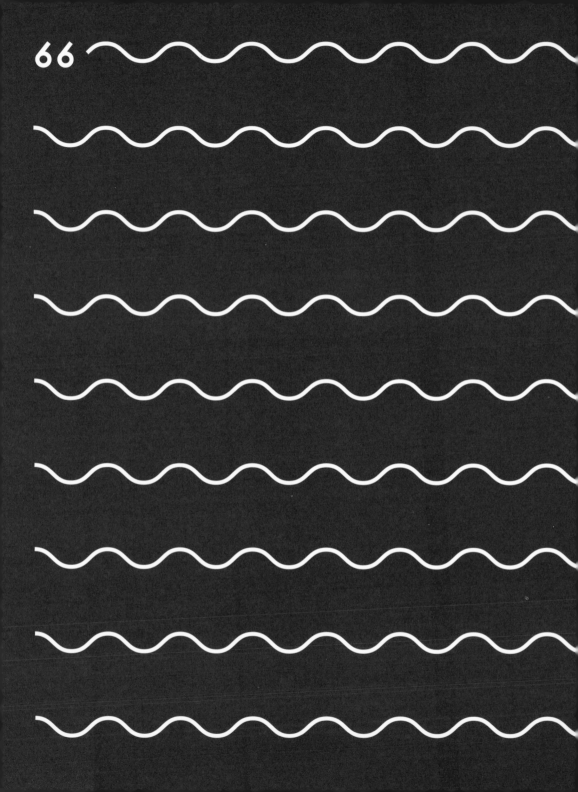

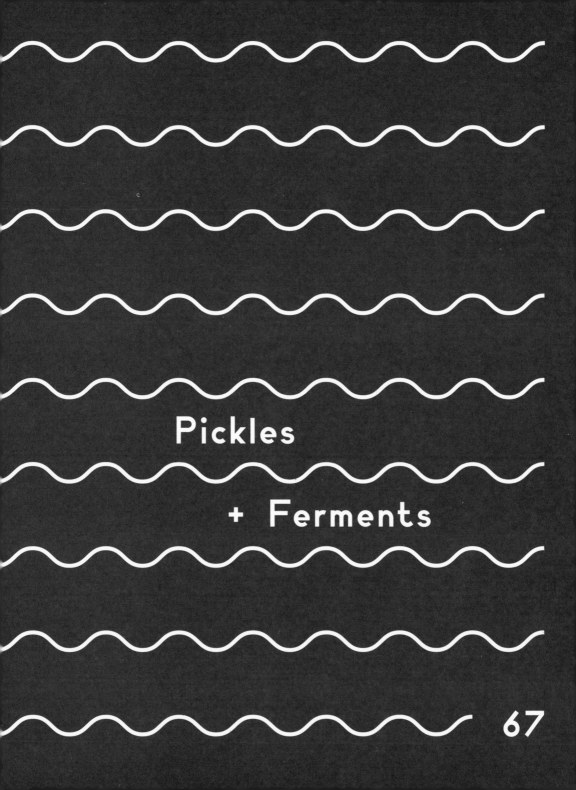

Pickles

+ Ferments

Pickled Cucumber

Makes enough to use in up to 10 bowls

Tangy, crunchy pickled cucumbers are the perfect accompaniment to any poke bowl!

- 3 small cucumbers or 1 large cucumber
- 1 tsp sea salt

Pickling Liquor

- 75 ml (2½ fl oz/⅓ cup) rice wine vinegar
- 2 tbsp sugar
- pinch of sea salt

Using a mandoline or a sharp knife, finely slice the cucumber into ribbons around 2 mm (⅛ inch) thick. Sprinkle with salt and leave for 10 minutes. Combine all the pickling liquor ingredients in a saucepan and simmer gently over a low heat until the sugar and salt have dissolved. Rinse the cucumber thoroughly to remove the salt, then drain. Once the pickling liquor has fully cooled, pour over the cucumbers and transfer to a sterilised jar. The pickles are ready to eat immediately, but will keep in the fridge for up to 3-5 days.

Pickled Watermelon

Makes enough to use in up to 10 bowls

Brine

- 2 tbsp salt
- 1 litre (35 fl oz/4½ cups) water

- ⅛ watermelon, rind only (but with a small amount of red flesh still attached), tough outer peel removed, cut into 2 cm (¾ inch) cubes

Pickling Liquor

- 100 ml (3½ fl oz/½ cup) rice wine vinegar
- 2 tbsp water
- 2 tbsp sugar
- 3 tablespoons bottled yuzu juice

Pickled watermelon rind is a revelation, and especially tasty with the citrusy tang of yuzu juice.

In a saucepan, bring the brine ingredients to a boil over a high heat. Pour over the prepared watermelon rind and leave to brine for around 12 hours or overnight. Drain and rinse before transferring to a large sterilised jar.

Combine the pickling liquor ingredients in a saucepan and bring to a simmer over a gentle heat, until the sugar has dissolved. Allow to cool slightly, then pour over the watermelon. Leave the pickles to mature for 1 week in the fridge. They will keep refrigerated for up to 1 month.

Soy Pickled Shiitake

Makes enough to use in up to 10 bowls

~~~~~~~~~~~~~~~~~~~~~~~~~~~~~~~~~~~

- 50 g (2 oz/2 cups) dried shiitake mushrooms
- 400 ml (13½ fl oz/1⅔ cups) freshly boiled water

Pickling Liquor
~~~~~~~~~~~~~~~~~~~~~~~~~~~~~~~~~~~

- 120 ml (4 fl oz/½ cup) soy sauce
- 120 ml (4 fl oz/½ cup) rice wine vinegar
- 100 g (3½ oz/½ cup) sugar
- 10 cm (4 inch) piece fresh ginger, peeled and sliced
- 1 star anise
- 5 Szechuan peppercorns
- 2 bay leaves

Based on the pickled mushrooms on the menu at Momofuku in New York, these shiitake pack a powerful flavour punch and pair perfectly with tofu and oily fish. Make sure you reserve the pickling liquor to use as an umami-rich dressing for salads, as we do with our Wasabi Salmon Poke (page 45).

Place the mushrooms in a large bowl and cover with the boiling water. Leave to rehydrate for 30 minutes.

Combine the pickling liquor ingredients in a saucepan and bring to a simmer, over a gentle heat, stirring occasionally, until the sugar has dissolved. Add the rehydrated mushrooms and their soaking liquid and simmer for a further 10 minutes.

Remove from the heat, discard the spices and transfer to a sterilised jar. Once cool, transfer to the fridge where the pickles will keep for up to 1 month.

Umeboshi Pickled Rhubarb

Makes enough to fill 2 small jars

Pickling Liquor
~~~~~~~~~~~~~~~~~~~~~~~~~~~~~~~~~~~

- 100 g (3½ oz/½ cup) sugar
- 120 ml (4 fl oz/½ cup) water
- 120 ml (4 fl oz/½ cup) rice wine vinegar
- 1 tsp umeboshi paste

~~~~~~~~~~~~~~~~~~~~~~~~~~~~~~~~~~~

- 2 stalks of rhubarb, sliced lengthways
- 1 bird's eye chilli, sliced

A very punchy pickle. Use finely diced in salads or with fish and reserve the pickling liquor for dressings.

Place the pickling liquor ingredients in a saucepan and heat until the sugar has dissolved.

Arrange the rhubarb in a sterilised jar with the sliced chilli. Pour over the hot pickling liquor, allow to cool, and leave to pickle for at least 48 hours. Store in the fridge for up to 2 weeks.

Umeboshi
Pickled Rhubarb
Page 69

Pickled Cucumber
Page 68

Pickled
Watermelon
Page 68

Soy Pickled
Shiitake
Page 69

Beetroot Pickled
Baby Corn
Page 73

This palate-cleansing pickle adds a fiery, sweet addition to our bowls. The key is to find young ginger. We like to add an umeboshi plum to add extra colour and tartness to the pickle.

Peel or use a spoon to scrape the skin off the ginger and slice it as thin as possible with a mandoline. Salt the ginger for 5 minutes to draw out the moisture. Then rinse.

Bring a small pan of water to the boil and blanch the ginger for 2 minutes, then drain and press to squeeze out the water. Put the ginger into a sterilised, airtight container.

In a separate saucepan, heat the pickling liquor ingredients over a medium heat until the sugar dissolves, then bring to the boil. Pour the pickling liquor over the ginger and let it cool, then transfer the container to the fridge.

The ginger will take a few days to pickle, but will last for months in the fridge.

Pink Pickled Ginger

Makes enough to use
in up to 10 bowls

— 200 g (7 oz) young fresh ginger (look out for the pink tips)
— 1½ tsp sea salt

Pickling Liquor

— 100 ml (3½ fl oz / ½ cup) rice wine vinegar
— 100 ml (3½ fl oz / ½ cup) water
— 60 g (2 oz / ¼ cup) sugar
— 1½ tsp sea salt
— 1 umeboshi plum or 1 fresh shiso leaf

Beetroot Pickled Baby Corns

Makes enough to use
in up to 15 bowls

— 190 g (7 oz) baby corn, thinly sliced into rounds

Beetroot Pickling Liquor

— 2 large raw beetroot (beets), peeled and sliced
— 250 ml (8 fl oz / 1 cup) water
— 125 ml (4 fl oz / ½ cup) rice wine vinegar
— 3 tbsp sugar
— 2 tsp salt

The beetroot (beet) in this pickling liquid turns the baby corn a vibrant shade of pink that has often led people to mistake them for flowers or raspberries!

Place the baby corn in a sterilised glass jar.

Put all the pickling liquor ingredients in a saucepan and bring to a simmer for 10 minutes, then allow to cool. Once cooled, remove the sliced beetroot and pour the liquor over the baby corn.

Leave for 24 hours in the fridge to allow the corn to absorb the beetroot colour. The pickles will keep in the fridge for up to 1 week.

Pineapple Kimchi

Serves 4 as a side

~~~~~~~~~~~~

- 1 garlic clove, peeled and crushed
- 1 thumb-sized piece of fresh ginger, finely sliced
- 35 g (1 oz/¼ cup) fresh pineapple, blitzed in a blender or grated
- 2 tsp Korean chilli pepper powder
- juice of 1 lime
- 1 tbsp fish sauce
- ½ small pineapple, cut into 1 cm (½ inch) cubes
- 1 carrot, julienned

This sweet, spicy and tangy relish uses Korean chilli pepper powder, which packs a punch, so add slowly!

Combine all the ingredients, except for the pineapple and carrot. Taste and add more Korean chilli pepper powder if desired. Stir this paste through the carrot and diced pineapple and transfer the kimchi to a sterilised jar. The kimchi is ready to eat immediately, but will keep in the fridge for up to 5 days.

White Fennel Kimchi

Serves 4 as a side

~~~~~~~~~~~~

- 1 garlic clove, peeled and crushed
- thumb-sized piece of fresh ginger, julienned
- 3½ tbsp fish sauce
- 1 tsp shrimp paste
- juice of ½ lime
- 135 g (5 oz) fennel, thinly sliced with a mandoline
- 1 spring onion (scallion), finely sliced

This kimchi doesn't use any Korean chilli pepper – although it isn't spicy, it still packs a flavour punch.

Combine the garlic, ginger, fish sauce, shrimp paste and lime thoroughly in a bowl. Fold in the fennel and spring onion. Transfer to a sterilised jar. The kimchi is ready to eat in 30 minutes, but will keep in the fridge for up to 1 week.

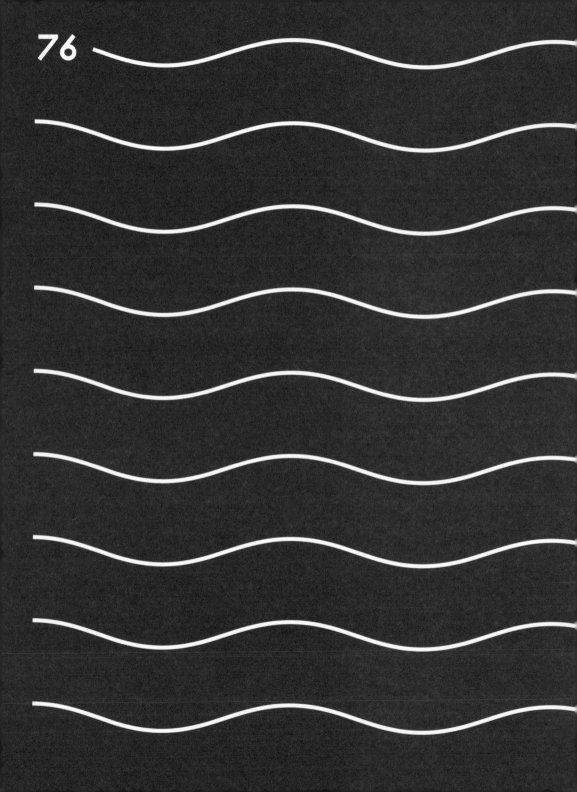

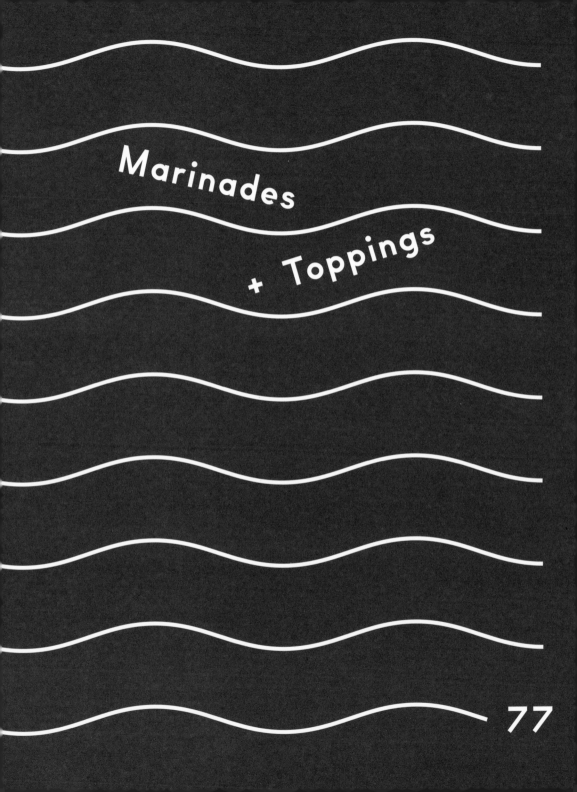

Marinades
+ Toppings

Spicy
Marinade

Shoyu
Marinade

Grapefruit Ponzu
Marinade
Page 58

Shoyu Marinade

Makes enough to marinate
1–1.5 kg (2 lb 3 oz–3 lb 4 oz) poke

This is our go-to marinade for seasoning most kinds of poke. Look for traditionally brewed soy sauce, or shoyu, for a more complex and rounded flavour profile. We also like to use tamari as a gluten-free option.

- 125 ml (4 fl oz/½ cup) traditionally brewed soy sauce
- 2 tbsp water
- 1 thumb-sized piece of fresh ginger, finely grated
- 1 tbsp sugar
- 1 tbsp toasted sesame oil

Whisk together all the ingredients until the sugar has dissolved. Taste and adjust the sweetness if necessary. Store in a sterilised jar in the fridge. This will keep for up to 3 days.

Spicy Marinade

Makes enough to marinate
1.5 kg (3 lb 4 oz) poke

Pimp it!

Add fresh red chillies for extra heat

- 100 ml (3½ fl oz/½ cup) traditionally brewed soy sauce
- 65 ml (2 fl oz/¼ cup) toasted sesame oil
- 3½ tbsp Homemade Sriracha Sauce (page 86)
- 50 g (2 oz) piece of fresh ginger, finely grated
- 1 garlic clove, peeled and crushed
- 4 tbsp sesame seeds, toasted

A fiery marinade made with fresh ginger and Sriracha sauce.

Whisk together all the ingredients. The marinade should be a fairly thick consistency – use sparingly to coat fish. Store in a sterilised jar in the fridge. This will keep for up to 3 days.

Basic Japanese Mayo

Master this basic Japanese mayo, then get creative with your own flavours or try some of the recipes that follow.

- ½ tsp sea salt
- 1 tsp sugar
- 2 egg yolks
- 250 ml (9 fl oz/1 cup) groundnut oil (or other light flavourless oil)
- 3½ tbsp dashi stock
- 1 tbsp rice wine vinegar
- 1 tsp bottled yuzu juice

Whisk together the salt, sugar and egg yolks in a large bowl for 1 minute. Gradually drizzle in the oil, bit by bit, whisking all the while to achieve a creamy consistency. Combine the stock, vinegar and yuzu juice and whisk slowly into the mayonnaise to combine. Store in a sterilised jar in the fridge. This will keep for up to 2 weeks.

Spicy Mayo

all mayo recipes make approx 250 g (9 oz/1 cup)

- 250 g (9 oz/1 cup) Basic Japanese Mayo (see above)
- juice of 1 lemon
- 3 tbsp bought or Homemade Sriracha Sauce (page 86)

Combine all the ingredients in a bowl before transferring to a sterilised jar. This will keep for up to 2 weeks in the fridge.

Wasabi Mayo

- 250 g (9 oz/1 cup) Basic Japanese Mayo (see above)
- 30 g (1 oz) wasabi powder, mixed to a thick paste with cold water
- juice of 2 limes

Add the mayo to the wasabi paste, gradually at first to ensure no lumps. Once fully combined, stir in the lime juice. Transfer to a sterilised jar. This will keep for up to 2 weeks in the fridge.

Gochujang Mayo

- 250 g (9 oz/1 cup) Basic Japanese Mayo (page 80)
- 40 g (1½ oz) gochujang paste
- juice of 1½ limes
- 2 tbsp mirin
- ½ tsp salt

Combine all the ingredients in a bowl before transferring to a sterilised jar. This will keep for up to 2 weeks in the fridge.

Black Miso Mayo

- 250 g (9 oz/1 cup) Basic Japanese Mayo (page 80)
- 50 g (2 oz/⅓ cup) black sesame seeds, ground to a paste
- 3½ tbsp Sweet Miso Sauce (page 89)

Combine all the ingredients in a bowl before transferring to a sterilised jar. This will keep for up to 1 week in the fridge.

Yuzu Kosho Mayo

- 250 g (9 oz/1 cup) Basic Japanese Mayo (page 80)
- juice of 2 limes
- 2 tbsp shop-bought or Homemade Sriracha Sauce (page 88)
- 1 tsp yuzu kosho chilli paste

Combine all the ingredients in a bowl before transferring to a sterilised jar. This will keep for up to 1 week in the fridge.

Lemongrass + Kaffir Lime Leaf Oil

- 4 kaffir lime leaves
- 2 sticks of lemongrass, chopped into 1 cm (½ inch) pieces
- 200 ml (7 fl oz/¾ cup) light flavourless oil
- 1½ tbsp sugar

Combine all the ingredients in a saucepan and bring to a slow simmer over a low heat. Simmer for 10 minutes, then take off the heat and allow to cool. Once cooled, transfer to a sterilised jar. This oil will keep for up to 1 month in the fridge.

Chilli Oil

- 1 tbsp Szechuan chilli flakes
- 250 ml (9 fl oz/1 cup) light flavourless oil
- 2 thick slices fresh ginger
- 1 garlic clove, peeled

Combine all the ingredients in a saucepan and bring to a slow simmer on the stove. Simmer for 30 minutes, then take off the heat and cool. Transfer to a sterilised jar. This oil will keep for up to 1 month in the fridge.

Shiso Oil

- 5 shiso leaves
- 500 ml (17 fl oz/2 cups) light flavourless oil
- 1 tsp sugar
- 1 tsp salt

Start by blanching the shiso leaves in salted boiling water for 30 seconds, then transfer directly to ice-cold water. Combine the shiso leaves, oil, sugar and salt in a food processor and blitz, then transfer to a saucepan. Bring to a slow simmer on the stove for 10 minutes. Take off the heat and allow to cool. Transfer to a sterilised jar. This will keep for up to 1 month in the fridge.

Lemongrass
+ Kaffir
Lime Leaf Oil
Page 83

Chilli Oil
Page 83

Shiso Oil
Page 83

Homemade Sriracha Sauce

The fresh sauce is fruitier and lighter in taste, while the fermented version overleaf has more body. We recommend you play with the flavours, adding more garlic, sugar or vinegar to taste.

Both recipes make approx
120 g (4 oz/½ cup)

Fresh Sriracha Sauce

Takes 10 minutes

- 150 g (5½ oz) jalapeño or fresno chillies, washed and roughly chopped
- 2 garlic cloves, peeled
- 1¼ tsp sea salt
- 1½–3 tbsp palm sugar or 1½–2 tbsp soft brown sugar
- 60 ml (2 fl oz/¼ cup) distilled white vinegar
- 60 ml (2 fl oz/¼ cup) water

Place all the ingredients into a food processor and blitz to a smooth paste. Transfer to a small saucepan and bring to the boil over a high heat, then lower the heat to a vigorous simmer and cook for 5 minutes. Remove from the heat and set aside to cool to room temperature. Decant into a sterilised bottle. This sauce can be kept in the fridge for up to 1 month.

Hawaiian
Chilli Water
Page 89

Fresh
Sriracha Sauce
Page 86

Fermented Sriracha Sauce

Takes 3–7 days

Place the jalapeños or chillies, garlic, salt, sugar, vinegar and a couple of tablespoons of the water in a food processor and blitz to a smooth paste.

Transfer to an airtight container or jar, cover with cling film (plastic wrap) and place in a cool, dark location for 3–7 days – the longer you leave it, the more acidic it will become. Give it a stir every day or so, remembering to re-cover it.

Pass the sauce through a strainer to get rid of the hard bits, then transfer to a small saucepan. Bring to the boil over a high heat, then lower the heat to a vigorous simmer and cook for 5 minutes. At this point you can add extra sugar or vinegar to taste. Remove from the heat and set aside to cool to room temperature. Decant into a sterilised bottle and store for up to 6 months. Once opened, keep in the fridge.

- 150 g (5½ oz) jalapeño or fresno chillies, roughly chopped
- 2 garlic cloves, peeled
- 1¼ tsp kosher or sea salt
- 1½–3 tbsp palm sugar or 1½–2 tbsp soft brown sugar
- 60 ml (2 fl oz/¼ cup) distilled white vinegar
- 60 ml (2 fl oz/¼ cup) water

Hawaiian Chilli Water

Makes 350 ml
(12 fl oz/1½ cups)

This classic condiment can be picked up in little plastic bottles at most poke outlets in Hawaii. Sprinkled over your poke, or just about anything else, it seasons while adding a spicy kick. This is a basic recipe — try experimenting with other spices or seasonings.

- 2 hot red chilles, such as bird's eye, sliced
- 1 garlic clove, peeled and crushed
- 2 x 5 mm (¼ inch) slices of fresh ginger
- 300 ml (10 fl oz/1¼ cups) freshly boiled water
- 3½ tbsp apple cider vinegar
- 2 tsp sea salt

Place all the ingredients in a sterilised glass bottle or jar. Stir well, then leave at room temperature to let the flavours develop for 48 hours. This will keep for up to 1 month in the fridge.

Sweet Miso Sauce

Makes about
400 g (14 oz/1½ cups)

- 250 g (9 oz) white miso paste
- 75 ml (2¼ fl oz/⅓ cup) mirin
- 75 ml (2¼ fl oz/⅓ cup) rice wine vinegar
- 1 lime, freshly squeezed
- 30 g (1 oz) piece of fresh ginger, finely grated
- ½ tbsp toasted sesame oil

One of our favourite dressings, bursting with tangy umami flavours!

Combine all the ingredients well in a bowl. Decant into a sterilised jar and keep in the fridge for up to 1 week.

Furikake is an umami-rich seasoning, usually consisting of seaweed, sesame seeds and other tasty bits and bobs. While available to buy in most Asian stores, it is a doddle to make. Here are some of our favourite combinations.

Furikake

Spicy Peanut Furikake

Makes about
300 g (10½ oz)

Use this as you would any furikake, to season and add crunch and texture. Just try not to eat it by the handful, as we may have on occasion!

Preheat the oven to 180°C (350°F/Gas 4).

Spread the peanuts out on a baking tray and roast in the oven for about 8 minutes until golden. Remove and chop roughly.

Heat the oil in a frying pan (skillet), then add the nigella seeds and toast gently. Add the roasted peanuts, sugar, salt and togarashi. Taste and add more togarashi if needed. Pour over the tamari, stir and remove from the heat.

Once cooled, stir through the shredded nori, transfer to an airtight container and store in a cool, dark place for up to 1 month - although it probably won't last that long!

- 200 g (7 oz/1½ cups) raw unsalted peanuts
- 1 tbsp groundnut oil (or other light flavourless oil)
- 2 tbsp nigella seeds
- 2 tbsp soft brown sugar
- ½ tsp sea salt
- 2 tsp togarashi powder
- 1 tbsp tamari soy sauce
- 2 tbsp kizami nori (shredded nori)

Spicy Peanut
Furikake
Page 90

Nori Furikake
Page 93

Crispy Onion
Furikake
Page 93

Nori Furikake

- 125 g (4½ oz/¾ cup) white sesame seeds, toasted
- 125 g (4½ oz/¾ cup) black sesame seeds, toasted
- 2 tbsp kizami nori (shredded nori)
- 1 tsp togarashi powder
- pinch of sea salt
- pinch of sugar

This is our take on a classic sesame seed furikake, always on hand to sprinkle over rice, fish, salads or anything that needs a bit of a flavour kick.

Combine all the ingredients and store in an airtight container in a cool, dark place for up to 3 months.

Crispy Onion Furikake

Makes about
185 g (6½ oz)

- 60 g (2 oz) banana shallots, peeled and sliced into super-thin rounds
- 2 tbsp plain (all-purpose) flour
- 3½ tbsp light flavourless oil
- 1 tbsp black sesame seeds
- 1 tbsp white sesame seeds
- ½ tbsp onion seeds
- ½ tsp soft brown sugar
- ¼ tsp sea salt flakes

We always keep a jar of this in our pantry, ready to use whenever we need it!

Toss the shallots in the flour, then shake off the excess. In a heavy-based pan, heat the oil to 160°C (320°F). Drop in the shallots and fry for about 4 minutes until golden brown and caramelised.

Remove the shallots from the oil with a slotted spoon and drain on paper towels. Meanwhile, toast the seeds in a pan over a medium heat, before mixing with the sugar and salt in a bowl. Take the fried onion rings and roughly chop – you want some almost powdered bits and some larger, crispy pieces. Mix these into the rest of the ingredients and store in an airtight jar for up to 2 weeks.

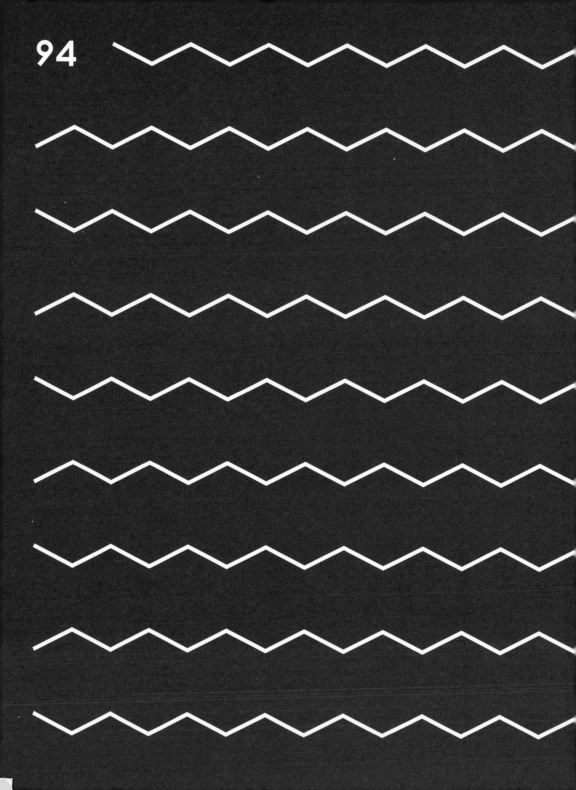

Sides +

Snacks

95

Pimp it!

add a few thin slices
of lotus root or
daikon for the last
2-3 minutes of cooking

Miso Soup with Enoki Mushrooms

Serves 4

- 500 ml (17 fl oz/2 cups) dashi stock
- 4 spring onions (scallions), finely sliced
- 5 cm (2 inch) piece of fresh ginger
- pinch of bonito flakes
- 4 dried shiitake mushrooms
- 125 g (4½ oz) fresh enoki or shiitake mushrooms
- 1 tbsp white miso paste
- 1 tbsp dark miso paste
- 1 tbsp mirin
- 240 g (8½ oz) silken tofu, cubed
- 5 g (¼ oz) dried wakame, rehydrated in cold water for 5 minutes
- few sprigs coriander (cilantro)

Delicious served as a starter to a poke feast or simply on its own.

Put the stock into a saucepan with half of the spring onion, the ginger, bonito flakes and dried shiitake mushrooms. Bring to the boil, then turn down the heat and simmer for 10 minutes. Strain. Return the stock to the pan and add the fresh mushrooms. Simmer for 2 minutes, then stir in the miso paste, mirin and tofu, along with the remaining spring onions. Season to taste, and simmer gently for another minute. Finish with wakame and coriander, then serve. Try pimping with a few slices of daikon or lotus root for added texture and crunch.

Crab, Seaweed + More Seaweed!

Serves 4

Mayo Dressing

— 4 tbsp Basic Japanese Mayo (page 80)
— 20 g (¾ oz) dried wakame, rehydrated
   in cold water for 5 minutes, then drained
— generous squeeze of lemon juice

Crab

— 2 fresh crabs, prepared by your fishmonger
   (use both white and dark meat)

Sides

— 4 nori sheets
— 1 tsp togarashi powder
— pinch of salt
— 200 g (7 oz) goma seaweed salad
   (a pre-marinated seaweed, found frozen
   in most Japanese or Vietnamese stores)
— 4 lemon wedges

This dish is all about subtle, sweet crab with salty seaweed, smooth creamy mayo and crunchy nori. A great plate to share as an appetiser – or if you're feeling greedy, halve the recipe and eat on your own.

Preheat the oven to 180°C (350°F/Gas 4).

In a blender, blitz the mayo, wakame and lemon juice until smooth. Transfer to a bowl and combine with the crab meat.

Place one nori sheet on a baking tray. Brush with water and press the second sheet on top, brushing again with water. Roast in the oven for 3 minutes until the nori crisps up, taking care not to let it burn. Remove, sprinkle with togarashi and salt and cut into wide strips.

Serve the crab on the nori strips with the goma and a wedge of lemon.

Bang-Bang Cucumber with Spicy Peanut Furikake

Serves 4 as a side

- 2–3 small Japanese cucumbers or 1 large English cucumber
- Spicy Peanut Furikake (page 90)

Dressing

- 2 tbsp Tabasco or West Indian hot sauce
- juice of ½ lime
- ½ red chilli, thinly sliced
- 1 tsp olive oil
- 1 tsp water
- pinch of sea salt

Crunchy and punchy cucumbers sprinkled with our spicy peanut furikake. Use in place of pickled cucumbers as a side to most poke bowls or a bowl of miso soup.

Place the cucumbers on a chopping board, then gently hit with a rolling pin to flatten and break up. Pull apart into small chunks with your hands or roughly slice. Mix the dressing ingredients together, then toss the cucumbers in the dressing. Serve in small bowls and top with a generous sprinkling of the Spicy Peanut Furikake.

Aubergine with Black Tahini + Miso Dip

Serves 4 as a side

Black Tahini and Miso Dip

- 2 tbsp rice wine vinegar
- 3 tbsp mirin
- 1 tbsp white miso paste
- 1 tbsp soy sauce
- 2 tbsp black sesame tahini

- 1 aubergine (eggplant), cut into 1.5 cm (½ inch) cubes
- 2 tbsp groundnut oil
- 4 tsp white sesame seeds
- 4 tbsp cooked edamame beans (optional)

If you can't find black tahini, white sesame tahini will be equally tasty.

To make the dip, place the vinegar and mirin in a saucepan and simmer over a low heat until reduced. Remove from the heat and whisk in the miso paste and soy sauce, then stir through the tahini and transfer to a small bowl.

Shallow-fry the aubergine in the oil over a high heat in a heavy-based frying pan (skillet) until tender and brown on all sides. Transfer to a bowl, sprinkle with sesame seeds and edamame beans (if using) and serve alongside the black tahini dip.

Hijiki + Edamame

Serves 4

- 25 g (1 oz) hijiki seaweed
- 125 g (4½ oz) shelled edamame beans
- 2 tbsp Sweet Miso Sauce (page 89)
- ¼ tsp toasted sesame oil
- 1 tbsp white sesame seeds
- pinch salt

A great little seaweed side dish. Hijiki is a staple in a lot of Japanese and Korean cooking, and we think it should be here too.

Place the hijiki in a bowl, cover with cold water and leave to soak for about 30 minutes.

Cook the edamame beans as per the instructions on the packet. Combine the hydrated hijiki, edamame beans, miso, toasted sesame oil, sesame seeds and the salt in a bowl. Transfer to a plate to serve.

Wasabi Slaw

Serves 4

- ½ Chinese leaf cabbage, core removed and leaves finely sliced
- ½ fennel bulb, julienned
- 3 tbsp Wasabi Mayo Sauce (Page 80)
- 1 tbsp black sesame seeds
- juice of ½ lime
- pinch salt
- coriander cress (micro cilantro)

This bad-boy Asian slaw is so simple to make and can be paired with most dishes. We also reckon this would work for other non-poke-related dishes; for example it would go down really well at a Luau with some slow-cooked pork. Dribble!

Place the cabbage and fennel in a bowl. Add the mayo, sesame seeds, lime juice and salt, and mix to combine. Coat all the veg thoroughly. Transfer to the fridge to cool. Dress with coriander cress before serving.

Hawaii's love affair with spam dates back to the Second World War and continues to this day. Walk into any Hawaiian supermarket and you will find whole aisles devoted to the preserved meat. Here is our homemade version of the popular spam musubi, pimped up with a teriyaki glaze, kimchi and pineapple.

Spam!

Homemade Spam

Makes one loaf

Brine

- 600 ml (20 fl oz/2½ cups) water
- 600 ml (20 fl oz/2½ cups) tamari soy sauce
- 150 g (5½ oz) sugar
- 2 star anise
- 3 hot red chillis, roughly chopped

Spam

- 1 × 1 kg (2 lb 4 oz) pork shoulder
- 300 g (10½ oz) ham, finely diced
- 2 garlic cloves, peeled and crushed
- 1 tbsp sea salt

Place all the ingredients for the brine in a large saucepan and bring to a simmer, stirring until the sugar has dissolved. Cool fully.

For the spam, place the pork shoulder in a large bowl and pour over the brine. Cover and leave in the fridge overnight to marinate.

Preheat the oven to 170°C (325°F/Gas 3). Take out the pork shoulder and discard the brine. Using a tabletop meat grinder (or the meat grinder attachment to your food processor), mince the pork shoulder. Combine with the ham, garlic and salt. Pack the meat into a loaf tin, pressing down firmly and evenly. Cover tightly with foil and place the tin in a water bath to bake. Bake in the oven for 2½–3 hours – the internal temperature should read close to 68°C (155°F).

- 120 g (4 oz/1 cup) short-grain white rice, cooked, seasoned and cooled as per instructions (page 25)
- 4 sheets toasted nori
- Nori Furikake (page 93)
- 350 g (12 oz) Homemade Spam (see above), cut into 4 oblong pieces
- 60 ml (2 fl oz) teriyaki sauce
- 80 g (3 oz) kimchi (store-bought) or 4 oblong pieces of pineapple, peeled and grilled

Spam Musubis

Makes 4 musubis

To assemble the musubis, shape the sushi rice into 4 oblong pieces, using the palm of one hand and the thumb and forefinger of the other. Place each piece of rice in the centre of a toasted nori sheet, and sprinkle the furikake over the top. Fry the spam in the teriyaki sauce until hot and crispy. Place the fried spam on top of the rice and top with kimchi or grilled pineapple.

Hawaiian Fries

Serves 4
as a side or sharing plate

Yuzu Mayo

- 250 g (9 oz/1 cup) Basic Japanese Mayo (page 80)
- 1 tbsp bottled yuzu juice (or substitute with lime juice and a little salt)

Fries

- 150 g (5½ oz/1 cup) tempura flour
- 250 ml (8 fl oz/1 cup) ice-cold sparkling water
- 2 litres (68 fl oz/8 cups) vegetable oil, for frying
- 1 fresh pineapple, skin and core removed, sliced lengthways into 6 mm (¼ inch) wide pieces

Garnish

- 1 tsp sea salt flakes
- zest of 1 lime
- 2 mild red chillies, finely diced
- ½ tbsp Nori Furikake (page 93)

We debuted these at Street Feast in Dalston Yard, London, and they soon became a firm favourite. A little bit like a pineapple fritter, with the savoury goodness of yuzu mayo and sesame.

Begin by making the yuzu mayo: simply whisk the mayonnaise and yuzu juice together.

For the fries, place the tempura flour in a large dish or tray with high sides. Whisk in the sparkling water using a fork or chopsticks until it forms a fairly thin, light batter. Be careful not to overmix – a few remaining lumps is fine.

Heat the oil to 180°C (350°F) in a high-sided pan or wok. Working in batches, coat the pineapple with the batter and deep-fry for a couple of minutes until crispy and golden. Remove with a slotted spoon and drain on paper towels.

To serve, pile the fries upright into small bowls or ramekins, drizzle with the yuzu mayo and sprinkle over the salt, lime zest, chilli and furikake. These are best eaten while still hot!

Lotus Root,
Taro + Sweet
Potato Crisps
Page 110

Spam Musubi
Page 105

Hurricane Popcorn
Page 113

Hawaiian Fries
Page 106

Lotus root, Taro + ...

- 1 sweet potato
- 1 taro root (available frozen from most Asian supermarkets, or just use another sweet potato)
- 150 g (5½ oz) lotus root, peeled and cleaned
- 1 dried rice paper sheet (optional)
- 1.5 litres (52 fl oz/6½ cups) light flavourless oil, for frying
- 4 tbsp sea salt
- 1 tbsp togarashi powder

Pimp it!

try dipping the crisps in Wasabi Mayo
(page 80)

... Sweet Potato Crisps

Serves 4 as a snack

These make a tasty and attractive looking snack. The addition of black sesame-flecked rice paper, although not essential, puffs up spectacularly when fried.

Thinly slice the vegetables, ideally using a mandoline. Break the rice paper into small shards and set to one side. Heat the oil in a high-sided pan or wok to 180°C (350°F). Deep-fry the vegetables and rice paper in small batches for about 1 minute until curled at the edges and lightly browned. Lift out with a slotted spoon and drain on paper towels.

Serve immediately, sprinkled with salt and togarashi or whatever seasoning you like!

Sweet Potato

Black Sesame Seed
Crackers

Lotus root →

Taro →

111

Hurricane Popcorn

Serves 4 as a side or snack

- 1 tbsp melted butter
- 2 tsp soy sauce
- 150 g (5½ oz) prepared plain popcorn
- 2 tbsp skinless peanuts, roasted and roughly chopped
- 50 g (2 oz) dried papaya or pineapple, finely diced
- 1 tsp nigella seeds, toasted
- 1 tbsp Nori Furikake (page 93)
- 1 tsp togarashi powder

This is our homage to the popular Hawaiian snack. It is salty, sweet, crunchy and highly addictive!

Mix together the melted butter and soy sauce and drizzle over the popcorn. Toss in all the remaining ingredients, transfer to a large sharing bowl and sprinkle over extra shredded nori to serve.

Crispy Togarashi Salmon Skins

Serves 4

- salmon skins from 4 fillets, scraped clean of flesh and blotted dry
- sea salt, for sprinkling
- togarashi powder, for sprinkling

This is a great way to use up fish skins that would otherwise be discarded. Serve in shards as a topping for poke, or as a salty, crunchy snack.

Preheat the oven to 180°C (350°F/Gas 4). Line a baking tray with baking paper, lay out the skins on top and sandwich with another sheet of baking paper. Weigh down the skins by placing another baking tray on top before transferring to the oven. Bake for 20 minutes until crispy, then sprinkle with salt and togarashi and cut lengthways into pieces.

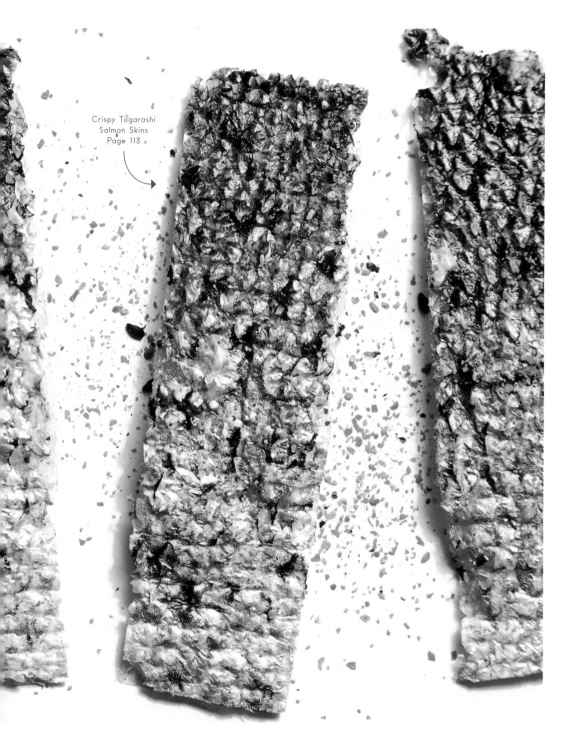

Crispy Togarashi
Salmon Skins
Page 113

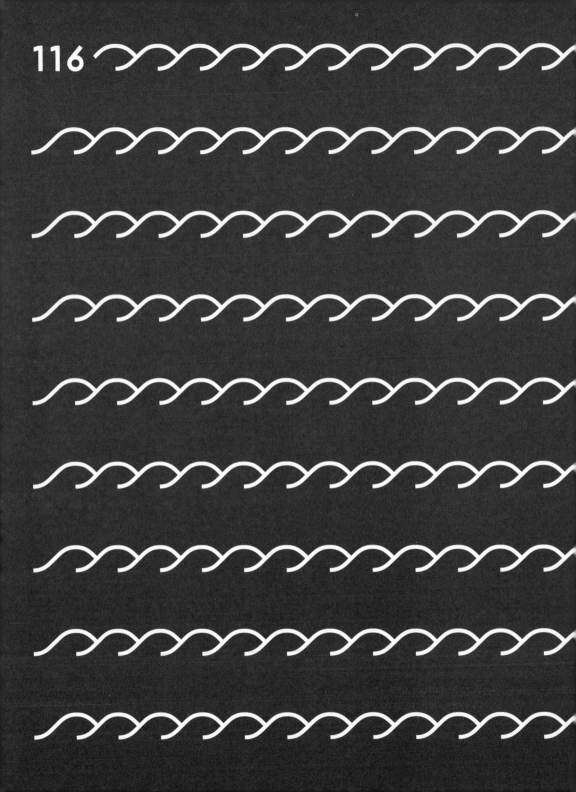

116

Sweet Stuff

Pimp it!

toasted desiccated coconut

—

black sesame seeds

Mango + Papaya Poke with Coconut Rice

Serves 4

Base

- 240 g (8½ oz/1 cup) short-grain brown rice
- 400 ml (13½ fl oz) tinned full-fat coconut milk
- 4 tbsp soft brown sugar
- pinch of salt

Poke

- zest and juice of 2 limes
- 2 mangoes, cut into 1 cm (½ inch) cubes
- ½ medium papaya, cut into 1 cm (½ inch) cubes
- ½ medium papaya, cut into 1 cm (½ inch) cubes

A sweeter take on a traditional poke rice bowl, with nutty brown coconut rice and refreshing cubes of fruit tossed in lime juice. It is worth adding a crunchy element here for texture such as toasted coconut flakes or sesame seeds.

Cook the rice as per the cooking instructions (page 25). Meanwhile, put the coconut milk, sugar and salt in a saucepan and bring to a simmer over a low heat, stirring occasionally until the sugar has dissolved.

When the rice is just cooked and is still warm, pour over two-thirds of the coconut milk mixture and stir through gently. Transfer to bowls.

Stir the lime juice and zest through the fruit poke. Pile the fruit on top of the coconut rice and serve with the reserved coconut milk mixture. Try pimping with toasted desicated coconut and some black sesame seeds.

Mochi Cupcakes with Yuzu Curd

Makes 24 cakes

These are inspired by the delicious sesame cakes served at local brunch spot The Nook Bistro in Honolulu. The glutinous rice flour produces a dense, chewy cake, lightened here by folding in whipped egg whites.

Yuzu Curd

- 50 g (2 oz/¼ cup) unsalted butter, cut into pieces
- 100 g (3½ oz/½ cup) golden caster (superfine) sugar
- ½ tbsp bottled yuzu juice
- freshly grated zest and juice of 2 limes
- 2 large eggs, lightly beaten

Mochi Cupcakes

- 3 eggs, yolks and whites separated
- 320 ml (10½ fl oz/1⅓ cups) tinned full-fat coconut milk
- 170 ml (5½ fl oz/¾ cup) grapeseed oil
- 2 tbsp black sesame seeds
- 2 tsp natural vanilla extract
- 500 g (1 lb 2 oz) glutinous rice flour
- 1 tsp baking powder
- pinch of salt
- 225 g (8 oz/1 cup) caster (superfine) sugar
- pinch of cream of tartar
- lime zest and edible flowers, to garnish (optional)

Start with the yuzu curd, as this needs time to cool and set. Set a bowl over a pan of simmering water, ensuring the bowl does not come into contact with the water. In the bowl, melt the butter with the sugar, gradually adding in the yuzu juice, lime juice and zest. Add the eggs, stirring continuously for approximately 10 minutes until the curd has thickened and coats the back of the spoon. Take off the heat and stir occasionally until cooled, then transfer to a sterilised jar and place in the fridge to set.

Preheat the oven to 180°C (350°F/Gas 4). Begin making the mochi cupcakes by whisking together the egg yolks, coconut milk, oil, sesame seeds and vanilla extract. Sift in the rice flour, baking powder and salt and whisk to combine.

In a separate, clean bowl, whisk together the egg whites with the sugar and cream of tartar until stiff peaks are formed. Take a third of the egg whites and beat into the flour mix. Then slowly fold in the remaining egg whites, trying to keep in as much air as possible. This will help the cakes to become light and fluffy.

Spoon the mixture into 2 greased 12-hole muffin tins and bake for 30–40 minutes until risen and golden brown.

Remove the cakes from the oven and leave to cool fully on wire racks before topping with the yuzu curd. Garnish with lime zest and edible flowers, if desired.

Malasadas

Makes 24 malasadas

Malasadas are a delicious Portuguese doughnut, made famous by Leonard's Bakery, in Honolulu. The following recipe was originally created for the Kerb third birthday celebration along with our friend, Tom Browne, who runs the New-Orleans inspired Decatur, in East London. We have featured two insanely tasty fillings to go with the Masaladas plus a highly addictive sour Li Hing sugar coating (recipes overleaf).

The Dough

- 1 tsp dry yeast
- 2 tbsp warm water
- ½ tbsp sugar

Dry Ingredients

- 1½ tbsp sugar
- ½ tbsp vanilla extract
- pinch salt

Wet Ingredients

- 400 g (14 oz/ 3 cups) plain (all-purpose flour
- 100 g (3½ oz/½ cup) evaporated milk
- 55 g (2 oz/1 cup) butter, melted
- 2 large eggs beaten

- vegetable oil, for frying
- 100 g (3½ oz/½ cup) sugar, to coat

To make the dough, first combine the yeast, water and sugar together in a small bowl, and set aside until yeast activates and foams.

Next mix together all the dry ingredients in the bowl of a stand mixer. In a separate bowl, whisk together all the wet ingredients then pour into the dry ingredients and, using a dough hook, knead the wet and dry ingredients together until smooth and elastic. Place the dough in a clean bowl, cover with cling film (plastic wrap) and refrigerate overnight. Alternatively, leave covered for 4 hours in a warm place until it has doubled in size.

On a floured surface, knead the dough for 5 minutes, then divide it into 24 balls. Place onto an oiled baking tray, cover loosely with cling film and leave in a warm place to double in size (approximately 30 minutes).

When ready to fry, heat the oil in a deep saucepan or wok to 190°C (375°F). Carefully drop the dough balls into the oil one by one. Do not overcrowd the pan. Fry for a few minutes on each side, until golden brown. Remove with a slotted spoon and transfer to a bowl lined with paper towels, to drain. Roll the hot doughnuts in the sugar, until thoroughly coated. Allow to cool fully, then pipe with your filling of choice (recipes overleaf).

Coffee Crème Anglaise Filling

Makes enough to fill 24 doughnuts

— 1 litre (34 fl oz/4 cups) French-press coffee (we like to use chicory coffee)

Crème Anglaise

— 480 ml (16 oz/2 cups) full-fat (whole) milk
— 360 ml (12 fl oz/1½ cups) double (heavy) cream
— 140 g (5 oz/⅔ cup) dark brown sugar
— 2 tbsp corn flour (corn starch)
— 4 egg yolks
— 75 g (2½ oz/½ cup) sugar
— pinch salt

Pour the coffee into in a wide, deep saucepan, and set over a hot heat. Boil and reduce the coffee until you have a syrupy mixture that coats the back of a spoon. You should end up with 50–100 ml (2–3½ fl oz) of liquid. Set aside to cool.

To make the crème anglaise, combine the milk, cream and brown sugar in a large saucepan, and stir over a medium heat until the sugar dissolves. Remove from the heat and set aside.

In a large bowl, mix the corn flour and slowly pour in a little of the sweetened, warm milk and cream mixture, whisking until smooth. Keep pouring and whisking until the mixture is smooth in consistency. Transfer the mixture back to the saucepan, and using a spatula, stir over medium heat until it reaches around 70°C (158°F) then set aside.

In a separate bowl, whisk together the egg yolks with the sugar and salt, until pale yellow in colour, and completely blended. Very slowly, temper the egg mixture by pouring around 150 ml (5 fl oz/½ cup) of the milk and cream liquid, slowly into the egg mixture and whisking. Once incorporated, pour the whole lot back into the saucepan and warm over a gentle heat, stirring constantly with a rubber spatula, until thickened. Once thickened remove from the heat and keep stirring until you get a lustrous custard or crème anglaise. Strain through a sieve to catch any lumps.

Fold the crème anglaise into the coffee mixture until fully combined.

To serve, carefully make a small hole in the side of the doughnuts, and use a pastry bag and small nozzle to fill them with a small amount of the coffee custard.

Pineapple Jam

- 1 whole pineapple, peeled, cored and finely minced or grated
- 80 g (3 oz/⅓ cup) sugar
- ½ cinnamon stick
- 3 cloves
- 1 whole star anise
- juice of 1 lemon

Rum Custard

- 1 portion of the crème anglaise (opposite page)
- 50 ml (2 fl oz/1 cup) good-quality dark rum

Spiced Pineapple + Rum Custard Filling

Makes enough to fill
24 doughnuts

To make the pineapple jam, place all the ingredients in a pan over a high heat. Bring to the boil, then reduce the heat and simmer until the water has evaporated and the mixture has thickened.

To make the rum custard, follow the recipe for the crème anglaise (opposite page). Stir through the dark rum.

Mix the rum custard and the pineapple jam together until thoroughly combined.

To serve, make a small hole in the side of the doughnuts, and use a pastry bag fitted with a small nozzle to fill them with a small amount of the pineapple jam custard.

Sour Li Hing Plum Sugar Coating

Makes enough to coat
24 doughnuts

- 2 tbsp Li Hing powder (available from Amazon and larger Asian stores or use freeze-dried raspberry powder)
- 70 g (2½ oz/½ cup) sugar

Combine the Li Hing powder with the sugar. Roll the hot doughnuts straight from the fryer to evenly coat in the sour, sugary mix.

Coconut Haupia with Pineapple + Mac Nut Praline

Serves 4

Pimp it!

edible violets
make a pretty
finishing touch

Haupia is a classic Hawaiian pudding of set, sweetened coconut milk. Here, the creaminess of the coconut is enhanced with maple syrup and vanilla and topped with a crunchy praline and slices of caramelised pineapple.

Begin by making the haupia. This needs to be done 3–4 hours beforehand to allow it to set and chill fully. Cover the gelatine in cold water and set to one side for 5 minutes to soften. Whisk together the remaining ingredients in a saucepan over a low heat. Remove from the heat and whisk in the gelatine leaves. Strain the haupia mixture through a sieve and pour into silicone molds or small glass bowls. Allow to cool before transferring to the fridge to set.

Next, make the macadamia nut praline. Spread the macadamia nuts and seeds over a lightly oiled baking tray. In a small, heavy-based saucepan, heat together the sugar and water, stirring occasionally, until a lightly golden caramel is formed. Working quickly, pour the caramel over the nuts and seeds, then sprinkle with sea salt. Once the praline has cooled, use a rolling pin to break up into pieces. We like a mixture of larger chunks and powdered pieces.

For the pineapple, sprinkle the brown sugar and cinnamon over the pineapple and caramelise under a hot grill (broiler). Cool, then chop into chunks.

To serve, turn out the set haupia, sprinkle over the praline and top with the grilled pineapple. Hot, cold, crunchy, creamy, salty and sweet – delicious!

Haupia

— 2 leaves gelatine
— 135 ml (4½ oz/½ cup) single cream
— 85 ml (3 oz/⅓ cup) tinned full-fat coconut milk
— 90 ml (3 oz/⅓ cup) maple syrup
— 1 fresh vanilla pod, seeds scraped

Macadamia Nut Praline

— 100 g (3½ oz/⅔ cup) macadamia nuts, lightly toasted and chopped
— 1 tbsp white sesame seeds, toasted
— 200 g (7 oz/1 cup) sugar
— 5 tbsp water
— ½ tsp sea salt flakes

Grilled Pineapple

— 1 tsp brown sugar, or more to taste
— ½ tsp ground cinnamon
— 1 fresh pineapple, sliced into 1 cm (½ inch) thick rings

Drinks

Shiso + Ginger
Lemonade
Page 133

Li Hing Martini
Page 132

Plantation Ice Tea
Page 132

131

Li Hing Martini

Serves 1

Li Hing mui powder is made from salty dried plums and tastes amazing. Adding this to the rim of the glass instead of salt gives a nice twist to an absolute classic cocktail.

- — 1 lime wedge
- — 2 tbsp Li Hing mui powder
- — 2 tbsp demerara sugar
- — handful of ice
- — 2 tbsp freshly squeezed lime juice
- — 2 tbsp Cointreau or triple sec
- — 60 ml (2 fl oz/¼ cup) good-quality tequila
- — 1 lemon slice

Rub the lime wedge around the rim of a martini glass.

Mix the li hing mui and sugar on a small plate. Dip the rim of the glass into the mixture and twist to coat.

Put the ice, lime juice, Cointreau or triple sec and tequila into a cocktail shaker. Give it a good hula shake. Strain the cocktail into the martini glass. Garnish with a lemon slice and drink up!

Plantation Ice Tea

Serves 2

This chilled tea is super refreshing on a hot day. It has a bitter undertone from the green tea and grapefruit, which helps to cleanse the palate.

- — 2 green tea bag
- — 6 mint leaves
- — 400 ml (13½ fl oz/1⅔ cups) hot water
- — juice of 2 fresh pink grapefruits, approx. 400 ml (13½ fl oz/1⅔ cups)
- — 2 fresh pink grapefruit slices, for garnish
- — ice cubes
- — 1 tsp honey or sugar (optional)

Steep the green tea bags and mint leaves in hot water for 4 minutes. Remove the tea bags and mint and allow to cool.

Once cooled, add the fresh grapefruit juice and mix to evenly incorporate. Leave to chill thoroughly. Serve in glasses, top with ice cubes and garnish with a grapefruit slice. If you would like the tea to be sweeter, add honey or sugar.

Shiso + Ginger Lemonade

Serves 2-3

Delicious as a non-alcoholic lemonade, the shiso simple syrup also makes an excellent base for cocktails.

Shiso Simple Syrup

- 250 ml (9 fl oz/1 cup) water
- 250 g (9 oz/1¼ cups) sugar
- 15 fresh shiso leaves, roughly torn
- 50 g (2 oz) piece of fresh ginger, sliced into rounds

Lemonade

- 2-3 tbsp freshly squeezed lemon juice
- ice cubes
- soda water, to top up
- 2-3 fresh shiso leaves, to garnish
- 2-3 slices of fresh ginger, to garnish

Combine the water and sugar in a pan and simmer over a medium heat until the sugar has dissolved. Add the shiso leaves and sliced ginger and allow to infuse over a very low heat for 30 minutes. Strain the syrup, discarding the ginger and shiso, before transferring to a sterilised jar.

When you are ready to make the lemonade, in each glass, combine 1 tablespoon of the shiso syrup with 1 tablespoon of lemon juice and add the ice. Top up with soda water and garnish with a fresh shiso leaf and a slice of fresh ginger. The syrup can be stored in the fridge for up to 3-4 weeks.

Acknowledgements

+

Index

Acknowledgements

Kajal Mistry and the team at
Hardie Grant

For finding us and having the
confidence in us.

Matt Russell

The creator of the our
glorious photography.

Ella Jackson

Who helped us start our
poke journey, but also
the master behind our design
and the book.

Ellie Jarvis

Wonder stylist with a
delicate touch.

Jacqui Melville
(Ginger Whisk)

Helped bring our vision to
life, through backgrounds and
beautiful bowls.

Nathan Perkins

Humour, assistance and
retouching.

Miriam Ibanez
and Saskia Gregory

For their playful, but elegant
ceramics.

Tom Browne

The Malasada man and also
the owner of Decatur.

Sam Richards from
Jonathan Norris in London

Our favourite fishmonger
ever! Thanks for all the
advice and fish!

Joshua Levy

For lending his culinary skills
to the poke test kitchen.

136

Acknowledgements

Ben Cooper

Such an amazing help on the shoot days – a joy to work with.

Paper Mill Studio and Wilder Studio

For allowing us to create a fishy mess in their beautiful photography studios.

London Union

We love working with these guys and girls and love what they are all about!

Kerb

For giving us our big break and all the support and guidance. Such a wonderful group of people with a great mission.

Fellow traders

All the traders we have begged, borrowed and stolen from. We owe you all loads – you know who you are!

Sophie Ridding

For providing continuous happiness and support.

Sheuneen Ta

For being the best host and giving Celia the ultimate poke introduction.

Team Poke

We really need to thank all of the staff and people that have helped us on our poke journey to date. You all made our days full of fun – very happy memories.

Our parents

Last, but definitely not least. Ros and Charles Farrar, Jon and Margaret Jackson for their ongoing support and generosity. We really could not have done it without you!

Nicholas Bash

Always bringing charm, energy and advice – big love.

Index

N

O

P

Q

R

S

Poke by Celia Farrar and Guy Jackson

First published in 2017 by Hardie Grant Books

Hardie Grant Books (UK)
52–54 Southwark Street
London SE1 1UN
hardiegrant.co.uk

Hardie Grant Books (Australia)
Ground Floor, Building 1
658 Church Street
Melbourne, VIC 3121
hardiegrant.com.au

British Library Cataloguing-in-Publication Data.
A catalogue record for this book is available
from the British Library.

ISBN: 978-1-78488-086-6

Publisher — Kate Pollard
Commissioning Editor — Kajal Mistry
Editorial Assistant — Hannah Roberts
Publishing Assistant — Eila Purvis
Photographer — Matt Russell
Cover and Internal Design — Ella Jackson
Food Stylist — Ellie Jarvis
Prop Styling — Jacqui Melville and Ginger Whisk
Copy Editor — Kay Halsey
Proofreader — Alison Cowen
Indexer — Cathy Heath
Colour Reproduction — p2d

Printed and bound in China by 1010
10 9 8 7 6 5 4 3 2 1

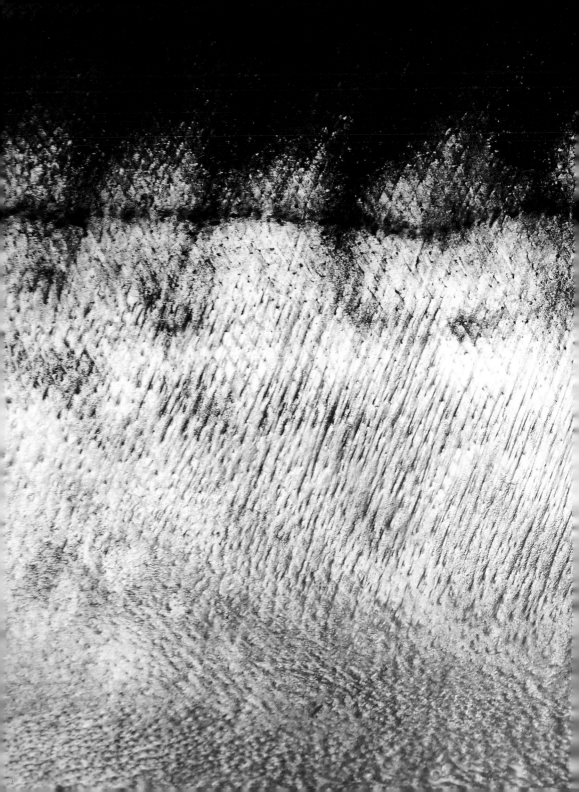